To Be An Entrepreneur

Just Get On With It

Miriam Dervan

**To Be An Entrepreneur
Just Get On With It**

First published in 2016 by

Panoma Press Ltd
48 St Vincent Drive, St Albans, Herts, AL1 5SJ, UK
info@panomapress.com
www.panomapress.com

Book design and layout by Neil Coe.

Printed on acid-free paper from managed forests.

ISBN 978-1-784520-93-9

The right of Miriam Dervan to be identified as the author of this work has been asserted in accordance with sections 77 and 78 of the Copyright, Designs and Patents Act 1988.

A CIP catalogue record for this book is available from the British Library.

This book is available online and in bookstores.

Dedication

Recognising where we've come from can be instrumental in shaping our future, which is why I'm dedicating this book to my Mum and Dad. As I look back on my life, I can see the essential role they played in making me the woman I am today. Their integrity, hardworking attitude, constant presence, unfailing love and unfaltering encouragement have given me abilities, aptitudes and talents that have been fundamental in all I've done. I wouldn't have started my business, overcome immense challenges or, indeed, added 'author' to my list of achievements were it not for them.

Sadly neither will have the opportunity to read this book, so I'm dedicating it to them as an expression of my love and gratitude.

This book is dedicated to you, Mum and Dad. Thank you.

Alongside my parents, I'd also like to share this dedication with John. You have been an instrumental, unique and remarkable strength in my life. You have done more for me than you will ever know. They say that a trouble shared is a trouble halved and a joy shared is one experienced twice over. You've been there for them all. Your invaluable support, loyalty, faith, confidence and belief in me has been indispensable and invaluable. I love you.

Acknowledgements

I'd also like to acknowledge the countless individuals who have supported, shared and shaped my journey. No one can achieve anything alone. I'm grateful for every single person who has influenced my life, but particularly those who continued to offer friendship, encouragement and put their faith in me through the toughest times. I'd like to thank you all. Without your contribution, MD Events would not be what it is today and neither would I.

First of all, I'd like to thank Brian Swindley for inspiring me to take that leap of faith. Without your words of encouragement I'm not sure I would ever have had the courage to make that first step on my own.

To June Pearce, my esteemed mentor, who helped me through the first 10 years of MD Events, I'm deeply grateful. You taught me so much about business and loyalty. I'm so pleased to count you amongst my close friends.

Stephanie Paterson, thank you for being our first employee at MD Events, for putting your trust in me and giving me immeasurable support through all those early ups and downs. Without you MD Events would never have got off the ground quite so quickly.

Thank you to Lesley Gould and Stacie Bradford for sticking with us and for reminding me of some of the fascinating people who have come across our path over the past few years and of the crazy adventures we shared!

I'm also grateful to Kate Sharma for helping me find the words to tell my story and share my passion and love for what I do. It was such fun to share stories over coffee and see the words develop.

Of course, I'd also like to thank my wonderful friends Kevin, Deirdre, Deniese and Carmel for those hours of 'therapy sessions'. As friends we've shed tears together, laughed a lot, but, most importantly, you were there for me. I can't express how important it was during those tough times of my life to have the unconditional support of such wonderful people. Never underestimate how important you are. You're incredible.

And finally, thank you to my two beautiful nieces Eve and Seodhna Dervan and my two handsome nephews Billy and Jack Dervan. You keep me grounded and remind me what life is really all about. For your unconditional love, affection and continued inspiration I'm so deeply grateful.

Contents

Introduction

Being an entrepreneur was something never spoken about, nor even thought of, during my years at school. We had career guidance teachers who, of course, wanted to steer you in the right direction. But entrepreneurship was a concept never spoken about or discussed.

From my own school experiences and what I learnt throughout my working career ultimately leading to my own business, entrepreneurship became fundamental in my mindset. My heart desired to write this book because I don't think there is enough emphasis on encouraging budding young pupils from secondary schools to university and third level college students to think about a free enterprise career. When I was at school it never occurred to me that one day I would be an entrepreneur. I never looked beyond my own capabilities at the time. Of course, I was young and most of us don't think that way. It is usually with experience along with life's shared wisdom the budding entrepreneur arises. But with some thought, creativity and by looking at what is around you, it's amazing how a career can flourish. All economies need entrepreneurs. They are the backbone to growth, to new opportunities, ensuring ideas, concepts, designs, notions, theories are all getting a chance to be heard, be seen, be created. We are the 'risk takers' of today and the 'thinkers' of tomorrow.

Following my own experiences, my desire is to spend time meeting young students and young people who have either not yet thought of entrepreneurship or perhaps may already have ideas about starting out on their own. I want to share my story with you to inspire, encourage or briefly enthuse you and give you a brief insight on how I got to where I am today and why I took the risk. I hope it may encourage you to think about free enterprise.

I hope to do this by guiding you on the importance of not fearing failure, disappointment or adversity. Sharing with you that the bad times are just as important as the good times, imparting the different experiences to encourage your plans and motivate you to think vertically and horizontally. The achievement you feel yourself, the sense of accomplishment while adding value to the business world, can be incredibly uplifting.

This book is sharing and imparting some of that passion. It is the risk, insecurity and lack of confidence which prevents any person from doing what is in their hearts, in their minds. But with a bit of encouragement and inspiration, it can change their focus from fear to excitement, leading to stimulating and motivating careers.

Chapter I

Recognising a different path

When you think of the word entrepreneur, who springs to mind? Alan Sugar, Richard Branson, Deborah Meaden? Chances are it won't be Miriam Dervan! Don't worry, I won't take offence. In fact, growing up I couldn't even spell the word entrepreneur, and I certainly didn't know what it actually meant.

And that's the thing: most of us don't really know what an entrepreneur is. We generally only hear the word bandied around on *The Apprentice* or *Dragons' Den* and immediately we think of big businesses built from scratch by ambitious and, at times, ruthless leaders of business. But being an entrepreneur isn't about wearing a sharp suit and calling the shots. It's about having the passion and determination to roll up your sleeves, get down to some hard graft and take the risks that come with doing it by yourself.

Now the dictionary defines an entrepreneur as 'a person who organises and manages any enterprise, especially a business, usually with considerable initiative and risk.' As you'll find out, I never really excelled at school so dictionary definitions mean little to me, but what strikes me about this statement is the fact than an entrepreneur can manage 'any' business.

So, if you take a moment to look around, I think you'll be surprised to see just how many entrepreneurs are on your doorstep. The couple who run the local shop, your plumber, the personal trainer at the gym, mobile hairdressers, painters and decorators, freelance writers, accountants, builders… wherever you look there are people working for themselves, driving their business, keeping accounts, looking after the team. Their office might not look like Trump Towers, they might not fly first class or have their own swimming pool, but these are people who are doing it for themselves and if you want inspiration, try looking a little closer to home.

My Mum

Now hindsight can be an enlightening, and also a dangerous thing. The first entrepreneur in my life was my Mum but, like so many things, I never fully appreciated what a fantastic businesswoman she was until much later in my life. My Mum started a B&B guesthouse in the early 1970s and continued it for a whole decade. Not only did she keep the house spick and span, ensure breakfast was on the table for the guests when they came down, she kept the accounts, managed the bookings and balanced the figures. She did everything herself while also bringing up two children and (in those days) she had to look after her husband too.

Her amazing ability to juggle so many different things was inspirational. My brother Niall and I never felt any lack of attention from her despite the hard work and long hours she put into her business. Whilst we always had guests staying in our house, it was still very much a home, and that's all down to my incredible Mum.

Perhaps, without even realising, those formative years of watching my Mum had a profound effect on me. I remember clearly coming home from school one afternoon when I was about 11 and going into the kitchen that was filled with the rich and delicious smell of Irish stew. Mum had had a house full of guests the night before so that morning she had to clean and tidy the rooms, do the laundry and refresh the house for more guests arriving that evening.

As I plonked my bag down on the floor, my mother was standing by the cooker in her work clothes, as she called them, stirring the pot of stew. Dinner was on the table at the exact time we arrived from school. Not only had Mum cleaned the whole house and prepared dinner ready for us, she had all the outside walls painted, the lawns mowed and her flowers pruned. We often talk about multi-tasking and my Mum was the absolute queen of it. Her time management was astonishing, her attention to detail astounding and the warmth she offered her guests was remarkable. Repeat customers poured into her business for years.

Over these years, as a child, it's hard to appreciate what is happening around you. Perhaps without even knowing it, she taught me so much in preparation for the business world: how to treat customers, how to time manage, the importance of attention to detail, the strength of managing finances, how to juggle many things at the same time without letting the ball drop. To the end of her life, everything my mother did she did well. That is key to helping your business be successful. I'd like to think that even if I had a fraction of the qualities my mother had then I'm doing OK.

Education

Whilst as a child I wasn't able to see my Mum's exceptional qualities, I was, on the other hand, acutely aware of my own shortcomings. I grew up in an era where you needed letters after your name to be considered 'successful'. Doctors, dentists, accountants and lawyers were the careers that carried with them real status and kudos. They were the coveted roles that we were 'supposed' to aspire to. But to get such jobs you needed to do well at school and for me, at least, that was going to be a problem.

I loathed school from the first day I started at the age of four to the last day I left at the age of 18. Those were incredibly difficult years personally. From the age of four until I left secondary school, I carried a queasy knot in my stomach every day and suffered terribly from migraines from the age of seven. I wasn't lazy or idle, mischievous or troublesome, and I didn't even have learning difficulties; I simply struggled with the world of academia. Learning things by rote, recalling information in exam sessions and the constant pressure of having to perform just didn't suit me.

I tried, I honestly did, and I have a distinct memory of a particular day in primary school, at the age of 10, when my class had to learn a poem off by heart. I came home from school with my head hung low as I knew the evening would be filled with me struggling, fruitlessly, to get the words to stick in my head.

Whilst it would only take my brother Niall half an hour to learn his poetry, I would be there for hours looking at the page, drilling it into my head, reciting it, re-reading it, writing it out, memorising it, reading it again, reading it out loud to my Mum, in a vain attempt to get the words into my head.

I vividly remember crying myself to sleep with frustration and fear as my mother comforted me and dried my tears. After four hours of trying, I just could not remember the words and I knew I was in for a walloping from the teacher the following day. No matter how much study I did, I felt that I wasn't good enough and that the school would penalise me for that. Back then, I don't think anyone cared how hard you tried, how much effort you put in, what other things you might be good at; it was all about learning, reciting and passing the exams.

Looking back, it's easy to say it was only a stupid poem, but the experiences we have as children shape us, for better or for worse. When you're young, school is your life. It's pretty much the only thing that defines you and your place in the world. As I said, doctors and lawyers were the people within society who were revered and looked up to and it became pretty clear early on that I would never achieve such status. So my self-esteem took quite a beating. Hating school and knowing I would not make it ground me down over time and led me to take a rather low view of myself and seriously limit my opinion of what I could do and what I'd grow up to be. Perhaps the worst of it was I did not tell anyone, not even my Mum. I just felt so ashamed.

If someone had told that schoolgirl with low grades and little self-esteem she'd own a multi-million dollar business, she would have laughed out loud for days. The girl who was so terrified of school tests that she felt nauseous most of the time, who narrowly scraped through her exams, who never even entertained the idea of going to university. The girl who beat ambition out of herself, who felt she wasn't good enough for anything, who felt ashamed and humiliated.

This girl would have laughed if you'd told her she'd own a global business and this, perhaps, is where the greatest problem was. School back then had just one measure of success: performance in exams. But the thing is, life isn't about passing exams. It's not about reciting poems or proving you can remember an equation. Sure, doing well in school can give you a leg up and open up more options, but it's not an end in itself.

There are so many things that keep the world turning and a lot of people believe if they are no good at school then they have nothing to contribute. That's just not true. I believe that all of us have talents and gifts within; the world of academia won't necessarily bring them out. Finding what you're good at can be like searching for daisies on a summer day, or like mining for diamonds. You can probably guess my experience! It took a lot of excavation to find my skills and talents, and perhaps if I'd had more affirmation and encouragement along the way, I might have found them a bit sooner.

First job

So I scraped through my Inter Certificate and the Leaving Certificate, which were the main school exams in the 1980s. With these qualifications I was able, at the tender age of 18, to apply for admin and receptionist roles. I knew little about what they involved but I knew that I was done with school, done with exams and done with reciting poetry, and that was enough to propel me into the world of work with at least some enthusiasm.

My first job was as a receptionist with a chipboard company in Dublin. No glamour there! But I loved it. Stepping into the world of work I felt I was leaving my old self behind, shedding the low self-confidence, the constant fear of failure and the endless futile quest to jump through hoops. Here I was given responsibility. I was in charge of the reception and admin functions of the company. It might sound childish, uninspiring, or even basic, but for a girl who ground all confidence out of herself, it was momentous. Someone actually thought I was good enough to do something on my own. I got stuck in from day one and was amazed I had no fear of it. I felt very grown up and knew I would love it – the total opposite of how I felt at school. I'd finally discovered the 'art of working' and it suited me down to the ground.

From the first day, as I put on my new smart suit, I felt like I was putting on a new self. I was like a caterpillar leaving its chrysalis behind and becoming a butterfly. I looked different and I felt different. I truly felt like I had become somebody in my own right rather than a lonely ghost in the shadows of school who was set for failure.

School had always been about isolated tasks: learn this poem, remember these sums, read this book. Work, on the other hand, was about a bigger picture. I never saw my role confined by the same restrictions I saw at school. I found it easier to see how everything fitted together. As a result, I was never a clock-watcher. At 5pm, if there were jobs that needed completing I'd pitch in and get them done. Not for overtime pay or to impress the boss, but purely because I found a great sense of achievement and pride in doing things right. I liked working hard, I liked being part of a team and I liked the fact that the harder I worked the more duties and responsibilities I was given. At school, my hard work simply produced frustration; here I could see the real and tangible benefits. Work suited me.

Pharma industry

As I mentioned earlier, the word entrepreneur brings with it all sorts of preconceived ideas, but it can apply to anyone, working in any industry. Some entrepreneurs are driven by a passion for what they do, others love the independence of working for themselves, and others just thrive on the sense of achievement that comes with starting something from nothing. Whilst some go on to become very wealthy, money is never the sole aim of any entrepreneur. If you're driven purely by profit, you're doomed for failure. It's so often the last thing that comes when setting up any business and there are always losses and sacrifices that come before any sort of financial prize.

Unlike other entrepreneurs who have a passion for music, architecture or inventing, I didn't have a passion for anything other than the sheer art of working. So I always think that my industry found me, rather than me finding it! I loved working hard and the sense of achievement that came with that and, over the years, I gradually came to believe that through experience, hard work and passion a person can succeed beyond their own dreams.

Having worked my way up through the chipboard company, my first job in the pharmaceutical sector was at the age of 20. It was with a clinical research organisation (CRO) in Dublin and I was only supposed to be there for two weeks on a temporary placement. Those two weeks turned into nearly two years.

By then I'd well and truly shaken off the uncertainty and insecurity of my school days and had come to love work. The pharmaceutical industry brought with it long hours, stricter deadlines, more compliance and harder graft, but I loved every minute. I started to learn a lot more about myself: my tenacity, the ambition I had inside me, the determination to learn and improve myself. I realised I could take risks, stick my neck on the line and make well-reasoned judgment calls. But these skills don't come on their own, you need someone to give you the chance to shine.

The first major project I was responsible for was when we were moving offices. I had full accountability of that project because my boss was based in the UK and there was nobody available in the Irish office to do it. I had to organise the entire logistical arrangements including dealing with lawyers, property agents and the company's leadership team. It was a lot to deal with, but I thrived on organising things, keeping track of projects, liaising with the very people – lawyers and accountants – that I'd felt I'd never be clever enough to work alongside. Most of all, I loved having a boss who let me just get on with things. It felt great to be empowered and not watched like a child. This project gave me huge confidence.

Following the successful office move, my first foray into the world of organising events came when I was asked to organise the Annual Global Leadership Team meeting for the CRO I was working for at the time. From the CEO to the entire leadership team, I had to organise all the logistical arrangements for their meeting and their full week stay in Dublin. It seemed liked a huge step up for me at the time, but I knew that the smaller things I'd helped to organise, like the office move, had demonstrated my capabilities.

At the time, I had no ambition beyond doing a good job, so every step was a great chance for me to prove myself. I learnt that in business you have to prove yourself and you have to be patient. If I'd been set on running my own business from the age of 16 I might have turned my nose up at the idea of running the reception desk at a chipboard company, or sorting out the shifting of tables and chairs for an office move at the CRO, but a lot of entrepreneurialism is about your mindset in the tasks that you do. In every job I've had I've always seen an opportunity to do things well and more efficiently. It's amazing how people notice not only what you do but your attitude as well. If I'd complained my way through the office move, I'm pretty sure that, even if I'd done a good job, I wouldn't have been given responsibility for the Annual Leadership Team meeting.

In fact, when I was asked to help with the Annual Global Leadership Team meeting I had no idea what event management was all about. I had to learn a lot on my feet but, unlike school, I didn't have to do it all on my own, I just needed to find people with the skills and talents to help me. There were no formulas, just great organisation, a willingness to listen, to collaborate with others, an ability to just get on and do things.

Of course, we were on a deadline, so pressure was high, but with a bit of forward planning and a few good contacts, things came together. Perhaps this ability to multi-task was something I innately picked up from my Mum. I thought back to the times I'd helped her change the beds, get the dishes washed or tidy the rooms to a strict timetable. Or even the evenings when I had simply chatted to the fascinating people who'd stay in our B&B, learning, without even noticing it, the art of communication and being able to pitch your conversation to make those you're talking to feel at ease. My mother always managed that effortlessly and I like to think some of her talent rubbed off on me. It's one of those essential qualities in business that no one ever teaches you, but it helps if you're lucky enough to be surrounded by great people who possess it.

Whatever the reason, I loved the sense of responsibility and I loved the sense of satisfaction even more. But through this experience, my self-confidence kept growing and I knew I had the ability and ambition to grow even more. The determination was there, the talent and spirit motivated me to keep wanting more.

What resulted was a successful meeting, so successful in fact that I was asked to move to the UK to set up an events department for the company I was working for. I jumped at this chance without a thought. I remember glowing with pride as I sat down at my new desk in London, with my new chair and my new phone. I then remember thinking what happens now? Nobody at the company had done this before so I had no one to mentor me, guide me or show me the ropes. I, it turned out, was the event management expert. How did that happen? What did I do next? I had no idea, but I was pretty excited about it!

The confidence the company had in me was encouraging and uplifting. I flourished in this environment. Just as I'd been given the space to grow on my own, so I now seek to help others do the same. Micromanagement does not work so give your team a chance to prove themselves and to breathe. It's up to you to manage them, not stomp all over them.

Going it alone

I threw myself into my new job with all the gusto and enthusiasm I could muster, drawing on every ounce of experience I had and gleaning information and pearls of wisdom from everyone I possibly could. Despite the responsibility and the buzz I gained from developing my own department, the thought of going it alone never crossed my mind until a chance conversation with a colleague got me thinking.

Brian Swindley was a trusted colleague who worked in the office beside me. We got to know each other well after I moved from Dublin to the UK. Brian was a very smart business person. He was clever and astute and worked on various strategies to enhance the company. I paid attention to what he said and we had some good discussions over the years. He not only knew the business and the industry inside out, he was honest, open and about as trustworthy as they come.

Brian used to come into my office every now and then until one October day he was sitting in front of my desk. He looked at the whiteboard in front of me, choc-a-bloc full of meeting schedules, potential clients and follow-up calls. It was a very different picture from my first day when all I'd had was a phone, a desk and a chair. We now had work coming thick and fast. I had built a department to help me cope with it all and things were going from strength to strength. Brian took one look at the board and asked if I would consider doing this myself.

He was amazed at the amount of business on the whiteboard. He said if this was the volume of business I could get for this company, could I imagine the business I could get if I was running my own company? It was a thought that had never even crossed my mind. Surely to go it alone you needed a wealthy backer, a rich uncle or billions in the bank? To be honest I dismissed the idea on the spot. I didn't feel it was something I could do without the support of the company behind me. It was just one great big risk. But his words never left my mind and over the next few days and weeks Brian's remarks kept creeping into my thoughts.

Of course it *was* a huge risk. Leaving great people and the security and comfort of a job I loved, but the idea of running not just a department but a whole company of my own stirred a great sense of excitement in my heart. The more I contemplated, the more determined I became. I began to see that just as the end goal isn't all about the money, so the starting point isn't all about it either. Money alone doesn't build a company; of course it helps, but you also need contacts, connections, vision, hard work and a deep-rooted passion to build a company, and I knew I had those. It had taken a fair bit of time to unearth those skills from within, but having started the events department from scratch for my current company, I knew I had the ability and aptitude to do it.

What I did next was perhaps the hardest and most defining decision of my life. Just before Christmas 2001, I decided to resign. That morning was nerve wracking as I took a huge leap of faith. I didn't have a business partner. I didn't have a company behind me. I was doing this alone. I woke up feeling sick – but not the kind of nauseating sensation I felt before exams at school, it was a jangling of nerves mixed with the butterflies of excitement.

That morning, I came to learn my first important lesson in business about decision-making. The second I placed my letter of resignation on my boss's desk I knew I'd made the right choice. Just making the decision in the first place is so often the hardest part. Once the decision is made you immediately move on to dealing with the consequences. If you don't make a decisive choice, you run the risk of spending the rest of your life eaten away by the possibility of 'what if?'

This was the start of something new! It was at that point I decided to 'just get on and do it'. Until then, I'd never truly believed I had the cleverness, nor such strength of decisiveness within myself. It changed my life forever, hence 'just getting on with it' had such an impact on where I am today. Without hesitation, I knew at that moment my life would change. Brian, perhaps without realising, was the first person to experience a transformation in my psyche. That was the light bulb moment; I chose to take the risk and start my venture.

As I've already mentioned, a lot of things help the world go round. Entrepreneurship is not for everyone and we need all varieties of talents, aptitudes and abilities to make any company successful, help individuals find fulfilment and to continue to push the boundaries of knowledge. But if the idea of starting a business from scratch and shaping and forming your own company gets you excited, then look around you and become aware of the entrepreneurs in your own life. Chances are you know more than a few. They won't be shouting it from the rooftops or ramming it down your throat, but be aware of them, talk to them, ask them about their own personal experiences and gain as much knowledge as you can from them. Everyone has their own story to tell and it's amazing what you find out about people if you just ask! I've come to learn that people are fascinating, complicated and exceptional. Never underestimate anyone and keep an open mind about them all – you never know what you might learn or how you might be inspired. You may feel you're not capable, but a crucial lesson I learnt was that everyone IS capable. Do not be afraid.

Thoughts to take away

"In any moment of decision, the best thing you can do is the right thing. The worst thing you can do is nothing." **Theodore Roosevelt**

- Look around for inspiration – it's everywhere.

- Opportunity is all around you, so make the most of what you have and where you are.

- Pay attention to the people you admire – take time to learn from them.

- You'll never fly unless you take that first leap, so go for it!

Chapter II

Have a business plan

Decision making

So there I was, my first day as a company director. By 8am I was downstairs, mug of tea in hand, with nothing more than a desk, computer and phone. I definitely had déjà vu. I was in exactly the same position as when I set up the events team for my old company – filled with enthusiasm about what the future had in store. The anxiety had been taken over by excitement as I got out my A4 pad and began making a list of all the people I knew. My next task was to start calling them and making appointments to meet face to face.

As I sat there with nothing more than a passion to get the business off the ground, you might have expected my head to be filled with concerns over money, getting clients, the uncertainty of it all, but the fact is the hardest thing about starting a business is making the decision to do it in the first place.

Decision making is probably the riskiest part of any job but it's also one of the most important and you learn that pretty quickly when you go it alone. Theodore Roosevelt once said: *"In any moment of decision, the best thing you can do is the right thing. The worst thing you can do is nothing."* And I have to agree! In business you don't have time to procrastinate. You need to have the strength of character to make a decision and go for it. We often place too much emphasis on making the right choice, but you need to understand that nothing is final; you always have options, even if you make the wrong choice. For me, starting my business was a risk, but if it all went wrong and after 12 months I was up to my eyes in debt with no clients, I'd just have to get another job and start paying off my loan. There's always a way out. Of course that doesn't mean you can make silly or rash decisions, but use your best judgment and *get on with it*. If you make the wrong decision, fix it and you'll only gain more in wisdom as a result.

I'll fill in the gaps in a moment, but one of the first major decisions that I did not regret was booking flights for a client without securing payment upfront. During the early years of the company we grew quite quickly. We started working with a client who gave us a considerable amount of business. We liked working with them, they liked working with us and everything was great. At the time the business focused on event management or, in other words, meeting planning.

Normally we get paid upfront so we can cover the cost of flights and hotels, which are the most expensive items on the bill. However, on one particular occasion and because this client was extremely important to us, I made the decision to go ahead and book flights even though we had not received payment. I took the decision because I knew and trusted the company, but when the money (approximately £100,000) hadn't arrived and the travel agent threatened to cancel all the tickets, I began to wonder if my decision had been the correct one.

The consequences could have been catastrophic. To lose those tickets would mean losing the whole event and the financial implications would have been huge. So huge in fact that I would have had to shut the door on the business altogether. But as I sat opposite the travel agent who was threatening to hit the delete button on our booking, I knew that neither the situation nor the consequences mattered; how I dealt with it was the key issue. To look back, you might think I was arrogant and over confident considering what was on the line. I didn't panic, I didn't stress and I didn't have nightmares about being chased by angry travel agents. I knew I could fix it, because I had to.

Perhaps you're sitting there wondering what you would have done, how you would have coped with the responsibility – not just to the client but to your team. Well, it's amazing the survival instinct that comes out in all of us when it has to. I believe there's a resilience and spirit inside each person that we draw on when our backs are against the wall. You will find a way. You will survive.

It's worth remembering that we all make decisions for a reason. So often in business you have to make decisions based on your intuition or 'gut feeling'. I'd certainly decided to book the flights based on my gut instinct about the reliability and trustworthiness of my client. Perhaps it sounds whimsical to base your choices on something as simple as a 'feeling', but the thing about intuition is that it's about much more than just a feeling. Intuition is formed by past experience, your understanding of a situation and your knowledge of the industry. It's often a pretty good gauge of whether or not a decision is a good one or not.

I knew I had decided to book the flights without payment because this was a client I'd worked with many times. I trusted them and I knew I could pick up the phone and speak with the financial director personally, if need be. I also knew that the hold-up had been created by the client and not by my team, so I could speak with confidence that we'd done everything we could to resolve the situation. When the payment came through after lunchtime, a few hours before the 5pm deadline, I knew my decision had been the right one and breathed a huge sigh of relief!

The thing about decisions that leave you sweating under the collar is that they also teach you to be wiser. They sharpen your instincts and your intuition and make you brush up your act so you don't find yourself in that position again. I don't regret the ticket payment incident, but you can bet your bottom dollar that we were on top of our game, and in the past 13 years of business we've never had a travel agent threaten to cancel our flights again!

Self-confidence

I must say I shocked even myself with the way I managed the situation with such confidence and that's really the key to a lot of decision making. What holds a lot of people back is the lack of belief they have in themselves to make and deal with the consequences of their decisions. You know the battle I had with my confidence as a child, but as I sat opposite the travel agent who was wringing her hands in despair and, indeed, as I sat at my kitchen table with a completely blank sheet of paper when I started my business, I looked back at my 25 or so years in work and thought of all the people who had encouraged me, given me responsibility, let me make decisions for myself and even helped me out when I'd got things wrong. I'd learnt an awful lot about business from those people but, more importantly, I'd learnt a lot more about myself. To make decisions you need to have the self-belief within you – and when you start to step out and put that into action, it's amazing what can happen.

What is a business plan?

So where do you get started? Well, once you've 'jumped ship' you've made the biggest decision you're ever likely to make in business. However, you've then got the task of steering your course to success, which is where a business plan comes in. In very formal terms a business plan is: a plan that sets out the future strategy and financial development of a business, usually covering a period of several years. In layman's terms it's all about deciding where you're going and how on earth you're going to get there.

Not wishing to put a dampener on things, but before you put pen to paper, it's worth pausing for a moment to consider a few of the main reasons why startups and small businesses fail:

a. There is no business plan

b. It's set up for the wrong reasons

c. Lack of capital

d. Inefficient management

e. Bad location

f. No online presence

g. Uncontrolled growth

h. Financial neglect

i. Lacklustre execution

j. Poor marketing

The list in itself may be enough to put you off the idea of starting your own company, but none of these things are insurmountable with a bit of planning and some careful monitoring, all of which your business plan can help you with. As you write, take into consideration the reasons why businesses fail and it will help keep you focused on your own venture and make you aware of the pitfalls.

As I sat with my mug of tea and my blank sheet of paper, I regret that I didn't have this list to hand or in fact the sheer fact that no one had told me it would be a good idea to commit my plans to paper at all! You might wonder how I can speak with any confidence on the issue of writing a business plan when I started my business with nothing but a passion and a list of contacts. But hindsight is pretty powerful and if I were to start over again today, one of the biggest lessons of my career and what I am encouraging you to do is to have a well thought out business plan. Perhaps your Mum has told you to 'do as I say, not as I do' before. Well, at the risk of sounding like your mother, that is indeed what I'm about to do.

When I started out I had a clear vision but I didn't even know what a business plan was or how to even put one together. It never occurred to me to physically write out how I was going to get my business started or what was going on inside my head. I had no idea what I needed, what financial support I would require or what the future was for the company. In my mind the business was going to grow to perhaps a small team of five people. That was my goal and I had no 'official' thought or plan on how I was going to reach that objective and certainly no idea of the financial pitfalls I might encounter on the way.

Even if you don't consider yourself to be much of a writer, if you think you're just more of a doer, or a visionary, it's still important to set out your goals in a formal document. It enables you to have a better picture of what support you need and, mostly importantly, it also gives you a clear idea of the potential costs and what financial support you need in order to sustain the business until you're funding yourself.

There is no set formula for a business plan but, roughly speaking, you should look to generate content around the following key areas:

- Mission statement and/or vision statement so you articulate what you're trying to create.

- Description of your company and product or service.

- Description of how your product or service is different.

- Market analysis that discusses the market you're trying to enter, competitors, where you fit, and what type of market share you believe you can secure.

- Description of your management team, including the experience of key team members and previous successes.

- How you plan to market the product or service.

- Analysis of your company's strengths, weaknesses, opportunities and threats, which will show that you're realistic and have considered opportunities and challenges.

- Develop a cash flow statement so you understand what your needs are now and will be in the future (a cash flow statement can also help you consider how cash flow could impact growth).

- Revenue projections.

- Summary/conclusion that wraps everything together (this also could be an executive summary at the beginning of the plan).

I'll understand that perhaps my word when it comes to business plans isn't enough, so I've suggested 10 good reasons that 10 different entrepreneurs, startups and small business owners have given as to why it is so important to write a business plan. Believe me, I wish I'd encountered them 15 years ago!

1. Clarity

Writing a business plan or putting together an investor deck allows you to think more clearly about what you are doing and where you are going. Key point to remember though is that the minute your business plan hits the printer it is already out of date, so don't depend on it as your to-do list. Think of it as a roadmap.

Paige Brown, BookingMarkets

What I think is key about Paige's comments is that a business plan is a roadmap, not the Ten Commandments. Like decisions, it's not the be all and end all. Life changes constantly. Your industry will change, technology will change, customer tastes change, your competitors and markets alter. If you're not willing to change the course of your journey to keep up with the others, you'll get left behind.

2. Gain a deep understanding of your market

Although it took several weeks and I've barely looked at it since, I credit my business plan for helping me understand a brand new industry in an extremely deep way before actually entering it, and for forcing me to examine deeply how we would fit into the market and what TalentEgg's probability of success was. As a 'risk averse' entrepreneur, it was critical.

Lauren Friese, TalentEgg Inc.

Sometimes it's all about the journey rather than the destination and writing a business plan will force you to think about things you may never even have considered. For me, I wish I'd taken a longer, harder look at my competitors. I was so focused on myself and my contacts that I didn't raise my eyes to see what was going on around me. Having a business plan means that, almost without thinking about it, you develop a sense of the bigger picture.

3. Organisation

The biggest reason to write out a business plan regardless of any financing option concerns is that it can help you stay organised and remain on track. Businesses without a plan can easily get off target, and revenues will suffer as a result. Creating a plan with expense projections, revenue forecasts and more can help a small business remain committed to its long-term goals.

Andrew Schrage, Money Crashers Personal Finance

As you know, school was never my 'thing' and so maths isn't one of my strengths. But when it comes to business you have to know your numbers. A simple profit and loss equation is the fulcrum for any decision you make. Most businesses incur losses before they start to make profits, but you need to have some idea of when you're going to switch into the black, otherwise it's like pouring water into a hole-filled boat.

4. Practice makes perfect

It's great to write one simply to throw it away. The mental gymnastics are great. The plan is basically worthless the moment you're finished – but it will force you to think about things you might not have otherwise.

Brent Beshore, AdVentures

My vision was to have about five or six members of the team planning events. I didn't think beyond that. What I didn't think about was the industries I wanted to work with, the risks there were, the opportunities there were. As a result, there was a period of time when I was more reactive, rather than proactive to the change that was happening around me. Foresight would have helped build that knowledge, which would have helped me make intuitive decisions.

5. Iron out possible kinks

Writing a business plan allows you to really think things

through. Your plan should question the validity of your ideas, the product/service target markets and so on. It should force you to do your own proper due diligence.

Nicolas Gremion, Free-Ebooks.net

Not every great idea is a great idea – trust me! Most ideas have elements of greatness in them, but you need to put them through the mill to make sure they really will stand up to scrutiny. Writing a business plan should help you to think things through and make minor alterations and adaptations to improve things in the long run.

6. Foster alignment

Writing a business plan is an ideal way to make sure that everyone on your founding team is aligned with the current and future plans for the business. In the early stages of a company, it's imperative for founding team members to be on the same page as to how they'll work together on moving the business forward to great success. Avoid any miscommunications by getting it all on paper early.

Doreen Bloch, Poshly Inc.

If you've got others on board with you, it's so important you're all pulling in the same direction. What can seem like a few small differences of opinion will only grow unless they're ironed out early on. The discipline of a business plan will help with that.

7. Hold yourself accountable

A business plan is a great tool that allows founders to articulate their vision and future plans for their company.

When using any business plan format, there are standard questions that force you to think and create a long-term vision and strategy for your idea. Once these are down on paper, they can serve as a guide to allow you to track your progress and hold yourself accountable for the future.

Aron Schoenfeld, Do It In Person LLC

A lot of people like the idea of starting a business because they won't have a boss nagging them to get on with things. Well, the truth is if you're serious about getting your business up and running, you need to have an even more ruthless boss – YOU! It's easy to get distracted by little things, like choosing the colour of the office curtains, and a business plan will help you stay focused and give you a real sense of achievement as you see yourself meeting your goals. A business plan will also stop you sticking your head in the sand if things go wrong. As we've mentioned, it's not set in stone, so you can adapt and alter it as you need.

8. Know your message

Business planning is incredibly helpful for describing what you do, understanding who your competitors are, and crafting a realistic three- to five-year plan. Each of these activities is crucial if you are looking to launch or expand a venture, and learning to speak concisely about your company will always be crucial no matter what stage you're at.

Garrett Neiman, CollegeSpring

You know what you do – but will everyone else? What often seems crystal clear in your mind can start to get confusing when you begin to share it with others. A business plan will help you to explain what you do clearly and succinctly so your customers and clients know what you're all about.

9. Establish benchmarks

Business plans are a valuable iterative document that can serve as a successful benchmarking tool. Where did your business exceed expectations? In what areas did your strategy maybe fall short? Whilst it's fine to 'pivot' your company based on what you've seen in the market, having something in writing puts the onus on you to be honest about your company's performance.

Charles Bogoian, Kenai Sports, LLC

Benchmarking might sound like a step too far when all you've got is a chair at the kitchen table and a phone full of contacts, but how will you know success if it bites you on the nose? How will you know when you're in dire straits unless you have something to measure against? All this forward planning will put you in great stead for the future. Remember too that it's easy to control things when it's just you, but as you grow you'll have to let others in on what's going on in your head. If you've already got it in a business plan you'll be making your life so, so, so much easier.

10. Confirm the maths

A lot of ideas sound great on paper and even in discussions. However, simple maths can make or break an idea. Before we launch any new idea, we at least create a financial model to project the ROI from several realistic scenarios. You can save a lot of time and frustration thinking through the numbers, and making sure it's possible to hit your revenue and profit goals.

Phil Frost, Main Street ROI

I'd like to pause and focus more on the financial aspects of a business plan because this is often the greatest concern for people starting out. It's also the greatest sticking point to the success of any business. Bad planning can break your dream. So I want to take the fear out of the finances.

If you've ever watched *Dragons' Den*, you'll have seen countless hopeful entrepreneurs enter the 'den' to pitch their business idea in the hope of securing funding and the invaluable insight and contacts of the leading businessmen and women. What you'll also see is some great idea fall at the first step, simply because the entrepreneurs haven't got a plan or any idea how much it actually costs to get their idea off the ground. Whatever your business, chances are you'll need some cash to get you started, and unless you've got savings or a funder already sorted, you're going to need a loan.

Believe it or not, banks are open for business and do lend to promising startups, but a bank manager, whilst less scary than the team on *Dragons' Den*, won't be inclined to shower you with cash if all you've got is a 'good idea'. You need to bring your idea to life and give yourself something to aim for. If this all sounds a bit scary and formal then remember the hardest part of starting a business is making the decision to do so in the first place. A business plan merely helps you to shape and hone that idea into something real. But it's not set in stone either, so don't worry about perfection, your plans will flex as your business does.

Now, I appreciate that numbers scare a lot of people – including me. The good news is you can get people to help you get to grips with them, but remember it's your business, so it's vital that you understand what's going on. It takes a bit of effort but, like most things, all that's stopping you is your own self-belief. You're more capable than you think.

Like with every other aspect of your business plan, your financials are a guideline. It's not about your balance sheet or cash flow results, it is an educated guess. Potential investors are going to want to see numbers that say your business will grow – and quickly – and that there is an exit strategy for them on the horizon, during which they can make a profit. Any bank or lender will ask to see these numbers to make sure you can repay your loan. Secondly, the most important reason to compile this financial forecast is for your own benefit, so you understand how to project what your business will do and how it will perform.

Your plan has got to be realistic. Think back to *Dragons' Den* – how many entrepreneurs have been laughed out of the den because their projections are 'over ambitious'. Be confident, aim high, but keep those feet on the ground while you stretch. Believe me, those lenders will know what they are talking about so it is important that you're sensible. Particularly if family members are lending to you, they will trust you to be honest and if your business venture does fail, at least they were aware of the risks beforehand.

Here are a few extra pointers for the sorts of things you'll need to consider when you're putting together your financial information.

Start with a sales forecast: Set up a spreadsheet with

figures that anticipate what sales you think you'll make over the course of three years. Set up different sections for the different items you're selling. Break your figures down into monthly sales for the first year and then monthly or quarterly sales for the second and third years.

Create an expenses budget: Whilst money is coming in, you'll also have money going out, and you need to understand how much it's going to cost you to actually make the sales you have forecast. Think about all the important things like equipment, rents, electricity, phone bills, admin costs, transport and your time.

Develop a cash flow statement: This will form the basis of your financial management so set up a statement that shows the physical pounds/dollars/euros moving in and out of the business.

Income projections: This takes your sales forecast and your expenses and puts them together as a pro forma profit and loss statement, detailing forecasts for your business for the coming three years.

Deal with assets and liabilities: You also need a projected balance sheet. You have to deal with assets and liabilities that aren't in the profit and loss statement and project the net worth of your business at the end of the fiscal year.

Breakeven analysis: The breakeven point is when your business's expenses match your sales or service volume. The three-year income projection will enable you to put together this analysis.

All of this may seem quite complex, and yes, finance certainly can be if you let it. Financial language can be rather off-putting but once you understand it at a basic level, it will stand you in good stead for the coming years. It is terribly important you know how to read a profit and loss report, a balance sheet and a cash flow report. I was abysmal at accounting and finance for many years, and indeed shied away from it. But if you don't understand your numbers, that will be detrimental to you and to the business.

If I were to start my business again, I would definitely learn the basics of finance. Don't be frightened of it. Only you can write your business plan, after all, it's YOUR business. Don't be afraid to ask for help. Don't worry too much about making everything perfect. And, most importantly, don't give up.

Thoughts to take away

You need to know where you're going and how on earth you're going to get there.

- Think about your future. Be ambitious about what you want and give yourself something to aim for.

- Put a business plan together – it will help you to focus your thoughts, think ahead, consider the risks, be aware of the competition and secure funding.

- Know your numbers. Finance is not frightening, but it is essential to your business. Taking time to make sense of your budgets and expenditure will put you in good shape for the future.

Chapter III

Know your market

I've often heard ambitious business owners claim that 'the world is my oyster' and 'everyone will want my product'. Well, not wishing to rain on anyone's parade, but that way of thinking isn't particularly helpful when it comes to getting your business off the ground. In business terms a market refers to the group of consumers or organisations that is interested in specific products. It's one of those things that might seem obvious but is certainly worth your attention.

The truth is not everyone will want your product, and even if they did, you can't possibly get yourself in front of all of them unless you have a budget the size of Coca Cola's. You need to know who your audience are so you can talk to them and talk to them in a way they understand and connect with. But every business owner wants their company to grow and knowing your market will also help you to look critically at what you're offering to see how you can improve it and also see how you can take your products or services to more people.

When I started my company in 2002, I assumed I knew the market. I had spent over 13 years in the pharmaceutical arena, specialising mainly in the research and development space. Following on from Brian sowing the 'open your own business' seed, naturally I only looked at the clinical research space at that time. Had I paused to consider some of the risks and threats within the industry, or even paused to look into the future to think what growing a business might look like, I might have made a few subtle changes to the way I did things.

When it comes to markets you have to decide whether you want to be a little fish in a big pond or a big fish a little pond. If you opt for a broad market then you may struggle to get your voice heard above the big boys, whereas niche markets have fewer players jostling for prominence. In 2002 there weren't many companies focusing on investigator meetings, so we were able to develop a niche within a niche, as it were, and cultivate our USP – unique selling point. I had vast experience, knowledge and inside exposure to the research and development world and as that was 'my' world it's how I got underway.

This worked for a while but, in hindsight, I should have broadened my vision. I was so passionate to get going I took the risk without adding that value to my future. I wished I'd learnt more about the market before I set off. Of course, it's impossible to know everything, but a little information can go a long way to giving you that broader sense of what's going on, who to watch and even how things might change in the years ahead.

I followed leads from ex-colleagues who were working for other pharmaceutical and clinical research organisations. At that time, there were no procurement departments so it was easier to win business, invest in relationships and secure client agreements. Vendors were chosen by the project managers so there were no lengthy tender programmes and everything was run on relationships. We grew quite quickly over the first few years and the business became quite established, but unfortunately only in the CRO and research and development arena.

As the years passed, we stuck to the life sciences spectrum rather than broadening our vision. A lot of business owners talk about their companies as they do their children and there are actually quite a lot of similarities. Babies grow up, it's a fact of life, and so should every healthy business. As it does, things will change, your role will differ, the way you work with your clients will change. All the time this internal change is happening, the world outside won't stay still and wait for you to catch up either. Just think of how life has changed in the last 20 years. Back in the 90s, social media wouldn't have been a consideration at all, the Internet was barely in its infancy and everyone used fax machines and carried cheque books. Fast forward to today and if you don't have a website, no one takes you seriously, fax machines are a thing of the past and life operates on a 24-hour schedule. You have to keep up or you'll be left behind.

I remember one day, finally sitting back and wondering why it was becoming harder to secure the deals that for so long had just fallen into our laps. I realised that the market was changing. Technology had moved on and what the market wanted was different from what we were now offering. Competitors who had kept an eye on their market were taking advantage, merging and acquiring additional services to enhance their own, using technology and social media to get the edge. Watching them broaden their horizons while we stayed still was almost heartbreaking.

So before you set out, stop and make sure you know the market and continue to stay on top of market research along the way. The good news is there are people and companies out there gathering information on trends, mergers and developments that can help you. It will benefit the future of your company, not just add value in the present. If you're not even sure where to start, I have a few tips to help you get to grips with the industry and the market that you're currently working in.

1. Are you in a saturated industry?

Saturation happens when you have done everything you can to reach the clients in your market. Everyone knows your name, what you do and you've probably worked with most of them. Eventually, saturation is what happened to meeting planning in the pharmaceutical sector. In a sense, we were too good at what we did. My competitors became only too aware of my business; they began to offer what we did and more, and pretty soon what had been a relatively easy marketplace became an extremely competitive one. The pharmaceutical marketplace was THE place to be.

As more funding poured into drug development and research, so along came the substantial budgets. Bigger competitors, who hadn't previously been in the pharmaceutical arena, got a sniff of the profits, saw the safety of the market and began to muscle in. Perhaps it sounds harsh, but that's business. Other companies were only doing what we should have done: seek out opportunities to apply their skills and build their business.

Entering a saturated market means you'll have to fight that much harder to get your clients, but don't let that put you off. You just might be the 'game changer' – and every industry needs someone to come in, shake things up and keep them on their toes.

For MD Events, we finally got our act together. This time, we took note of what our clients actually wanted, rather than forcing on them the same services and products that they'd wanted 15 years ago. We rebranded, became more technologically focused, and put together a 'white glove service' rather than the off-the-peg production line that we'd been used to. By relaunching ourselves, it empowered us to draw more attention to our business, plus we didn't stay stale for our current clients.

2. Use all your support systems in getting to know your market and using it in your business

Today it's easier than ever to understand your market and focus your products and services on their needs. With the Internet, so much of that information is at your fingertips through search engines, social media, press, product reports and industry news.

For me, the most valuable way to know what's going on is to speak with people already in your marketplace. There's nothing quite like a face to face conversation to glean what's going on and what's important. Ultimately, you're there to help your customers and clients solve their problems, so you'll find they want to talk to you. It's those people who will give ideas for your business and that's paramount.

Over the years, I was somewhat fearful of social media. Actually, to this day I am not personally on Facebook, Twitter or any other form of media except for LinkedIn – but my business is and there is an experienced marketer keeping all that up to date while also keeping an eye on what's going on in the arena. Social media has quickly become one of the most used tools for market research, so to not be there would be foolish, to say the least.

And, as ridiculous as it might sound, I was quite opposed to investing in the website, believing that was only information-led rather than generating business. I know it sounds crazy in a world where the web is the first port of call for everything, but that just wasn't part of my experience, and chances are, the next big thing won't necessarily be part of yours either.

But, as I keep saying, running a business is a journey that needs to flex and change as the world around you and the needs of your clients and customers do. The lesson learnt is never be afraid of what is happening today and beyond. It could positively change your business for the better in ways you never knew possible. Always keep an open mind, look outside the box and try not to fear what new technology is lurking around the corner. Make it work for you.

3. Be aware of your own strengths and weaknesses

In business you have to be honest. We'd all like to think we can do everything with excellence, but the fact is we can't – and that's OK. You need to think about positioning your company within your market so you build your business on your strengths. Remember that you cannot be all things to all people, and you certainly don't want to be a Jack of All Trades but a Master of None.

Don't try to be who you're not, don't try to deliver on a service or product you know nothing about. If you've taken the time to put together a business plan, you should have a good idea of where your strengths lie. Look to what you are good at, what gives you the love and passion to take the risk and own your own business. In my own business, our core competency was event, delegate and venue management. I also had a great black book of contacts and a good knowledge of who was who in the industry. These helped get me started quite quickly.

When you run your own business it's essential that you're honest about what you can and can't do. No one will thank you for doing a job badly. We had to be honest with ourselves that we did not know anything about audio-visual production so we found people we could outsource that to so we could offer our clients a seamless service. You already know that numbers weren't my thing either, so I got help here too. If I'm honest, I truly should have paid more attention to understanding it myself. But that's the power of hindsight!

4. Who are your clientele?

Perhaps the most obvious question on the lips of every business owner is: Who are my customers? It might seem obvious to you, but it's amazing how many businesses are pitching their services and products incorrectly. If you're a business-to-business company then not only do you need to consider which companies you're aiming at, but also which individuals within those companies you need to speak to.

When I started my business, I remember taking out my A4 writing pad and writing down the names of the people I knew. I followed those contacts, won business and ultimately kept to a select few, which allowed me to get on my feet and lay a firm foundation for the business.

Over the years, the contact base grew but knowing my clientele was an important factor. Who are you aiming for? Why them? Are they in the correct industry? Is it the right person you are approaching? Are they the decision makers? The scattergun approach does not work so it's important to do some research into understanding what clients/companies want and how you can help them.

There are also subtleties within the industry. As I'll explain later, not every client is a 'good' client and some research will help you unearth the ones to steer clear of. Who are those who are the resource eaters, reputation destroyers or bad payers? It's important to understand all these aspects because the wrong client can make or break you.

5. Ask yourself if you are in a growth industry

The aim of any business is to grow, so you need to take a long hard look at the industry you're entering. Whilst you won't find much competition in the facsimile machine industry, you won't find much growth either, so unless you want to go bust in a few years' time, best steer clear. 'Environmentally friendly', 'paperless', 'carbon free' are the new buzzwords of today and, hence, printing companies for instance are diminishing.

Don't just think of what you have to offer, think about how you're going to offer it to your clients. Do your clients need or expect to see your products on show or come in to speak to an adviser in a shiny office, or will your website be their first port of call? These are the kinds of questions you need to ask yourself to make sure that not only what you are offering is something people will want but also that the way you are offering it meets their needs too. Market research on your product or service should tell you how the future is looking for whatever you are offering.

6. Know your competition

When I started out I didn't know my competitors at all; I knew of a few meeting agencies and that was it. I was so focused on my business and my plan that I forgot there were other people fighting for business too. If truth be told, there were plenty more competitors in the marketplace than I realised. In the end the competition caught up with me.

One day I was sitting at my desk focused on my clients and the next week I looked up to discover that my clients were surrounded by shinier, more modern competitors offering all sorts of technologies and benefits I'd not even considered. My clients became seduced by these offerings and, quite frankly, who could've blamed them? Always watch what your competitors are doing, how they are advancing, what they are doing to make your clients want to work with them instead of you.

This is where market research is so important, make an effort to go to trade fairs to see what the competition is offering, ask your clients what their priorities are, dip into social media to see what the trends are and be bold about making decisions about the future. They won't always be the right ones, but if you don't at least attempt to stay ahead of the game you will most definitely fall behind.

Thoughts to take away

In business nothing stands still. You need to know what's going on in your market, or run the risk of being left behind.

- Understand your industry inside out, so you know how to position yourself in relation to your competitors, what to offer to your clients and areas of growth that you need to keep an eye on.

- Know your own strengths and weaknesses. None of us are perfect, but you can't play to your strengths or get help with your weaknesses unless you know what they are.

- Get to know your clients – not just who they are and what they do, but what's going on in their world. If you know their biggest challenges, you can help resolve them.

Chapter IV

Competitors are knocking on the same door

The word competitor often scares people. They can become 'the enemy', the other guys out there waiting to steal your clients. Well, let me tell you that whilst they're vying for the same business, they're not the enemy. In the London Olympics in 2012, the final of the 100m was won, as we all know, by the impressive talent of Usain Bolt. Next to him on the podium wearing a silver medal round his neck was Yohan Blake, a fellow Jamaican deemed to be Bolt's greatest rival in the final.

Whilst on the August day the two were rivals – competitors vying for the same prize – off the track they were training partners. They worked out together, pushed each other to the limit and challenged each other to aim higher, be better and achieve more. And that's exactly what your competitors can do for you.

I'm not suggesting you cosy up with them per se, but just as Blake and Bolt spurred each other on to become better athletes, so you should see your competitors as aides to help your company be better at whatever it is you do. Don't fear them – they can really help you out.

It's a lesson I wish I'd heeded when I started MD Events. At the start competitors never concerned me. I'd made the decision to 'just get on' and so I focused on my business and my clients. It's true that the only thing you can change is yourself, but that doesn't mean you can ignore what's going on around you. I did absolutely no competitive market research or analysis. I knew my business and knew that there weren't too many other meeting planning companies who focused solely on clinical research meetings in the pharmaceutical marketplace, so I found a niche and just set my mind to getting it started. I was not fearful of other meeting planning agencies who were well established and who were providing similar services to my own because, to be honest, I didn't know who they were. As a result, it didn't even cross my mind that they might be able to help me. Oh how I wish it had! The thing about your competitors is that, like every other area of business, things constantly change. Competition doesn't always come from the most expected places, so you need 360 degree vision to see what's going on.

1. Direct competitors

These are, perhaps, the most obvious competition. They are the companies who offer similar products or services and revenue goals as your own. Basically they make money from doing the same thing as you do. We have competitors who are on a par with us: similar size, similar revenue and turnover, same service. If you want an example just think of the big airlines: British Airways and Virgin. They offer roughly the same service with comparable turnover and market share.

Because there are so many similarities between you and your direct competitors, you need to find a way to differentiate yourself. It's what people often call their USP – unique selling point. It's a way of standing out against the crowd. For example, British Airways conjures up images of a professional, reliable and traditional airline. Think Virgin on the other hand and a more irreverent, glamorous and fun experience is likely to spring to mind. Without a key USP, you run the risk of fading into the background.

Once you've differentiated yourself from your direct competitors, make sure you also keep them close at hand. Remember, just as Yohan Blake kept Usain Bolt sharp, so your competitors will also ensure that you don't lag behind. One example might be the great home delivery revolution in grocery shopping. Can you remember when the big supermarkets started to allow customers to order on line and deliver to the door? When one started to do it, the rest *had* to follow suit or run the risk of incurring massive losses as customers changed allegiance. The same goes for online banking. There are some situations where you have to 'keep up with the Joneses'. If your competitors are offering something new that your clients want, you need to make sure it's on your radar too, or you run the risk of completely missing out.

2. Indirect competitors

Whilst direct competitors are the easiest to spot and keep tabs on, they're not the only ones you need to be aware of. You may find your greatest competitors come from areas you really didn't expect.

Your indirect competitors are the companies who offer similar products or services but have different revenue goals from your own. Indirect competitors offer the same service or product but have a different approach to how they drive their revenue. If we think back to the supermarkets and their click and deliver service, you may remember that the first player in the market wasn't one of the big shops at all. Ocado were actually the first ones delivering to the door back in 2002 and they didn't have a single grocery store in the country. No one saw them coming, but the others had to rally their teams to keep up.

To be honest, completely new players in the market are usually quite rare unless, like Ocado, they offer something 'game changing'. Most indirect competition will come from companies who have diversified to offer products and services you might not immediately associate with them. Again, the supermarkets are a great example, muscling in on the banking and insurance industries alongside their usual offering of bread and milk.

For us, competition came in the form of huge companies like American Express (AMEX), a global powerhouse with very deep pockets. Although AMEX is primarily a travel agent, part of their portfolio is to organise meetings as well. Large corporate organisations that spend millions of pounds generally tend to use these types of 'production line' agencies. They drive their revenue using a low price, high volume model – 'stack 'em high, sell 'em cheap' if you like.

As a small, niche, bespoke, personal organisation, we wouldn't class them as a direct competitor. Our service was more aligned to the small to medium clients who wanted a more personal, white glove approach. However, as clients look to make budget savings, the likes of AMEX can turn heads.

3. Replacement competitors

The third and perhaps most complicated competitor to keep an eye out for is the substitute. These are companies that can substitute your service or product for the same end result. In the world of business, this might mean that instead of having a face to face meeting, a company substitutes it for a webcast – cutting us out altogether.

I believe now, through many years of experience and wisdom, that these types of competitors are probably the most difficult and challenging. You definitely need to be on your guard at all times. They will change the scope of the market and will move products and services to a different level before anyone can take a breath.

Apple is an excellent example of this within the communication technology industry. For ages Nokia was head and shoulders above the rest when it came to mobile technology. Then along came Apple with their all-singing, all-dancing iPhone and knocked everyone else out of the park. The technology they had, their synchronisation across platforms and integration with different media such as iTunes, gave customers different expectations and experiences. What's even more impressive is how they have managed to maintain that momentum. Every year they are updating and improving what they provide. Their competitors just can't keep up. No one else has been able to develop anything on a par. Apple is known as a constant replacement competitor.

Sometimes these replacement competitors also rise out of the blue. I remember a client we worked with early on. They were a global organisation and we worked tirelessly with their project teams. We had quarterly meetings with them, demonstrating our cost reductions, cost avoidances, the overall savings made, the high quality delivery of our service and reviewing all the KPIs which went with the management of that account.

We had a great relationship, exceeded expectations, did everything right and were sailing along nicely – or so we thought. Then, one day, we'd finished sharing the latest round of great stats and were feeling pretty pleased with ourselves, when the blow came. They no longer needed our services on a regular basis. We were shocked, stunned. Nothing had gone wrong. The figures were all great. Everyone had been so happy. Who was going to organise the meetings now? Who were the competitors who could do a better job than us?

The answer: them. The company had decided to set up an internal department that would be securing most of their business from now on, keeping everything in house under one roof. We were stunned. None of us had seen this coming.

To be honest I'm not sure there's much we could have done about it, but we have certainly made a point going forward to make ourselves an invaluable asset to our clients. You can never get too comfortable or rest on your laurels. The key to avoiding the unexpected competitors is to find ways to go above and beyond the call of duty to suggest improvements, efficiencies and innovation.

Another thing this taught us was the lesson about putting all our eggs in one basket. This was a huge account for us at the time and in an instant it was gone. Nothing is ever certain in business, clients come and go like the wind, competitors spring up from nowhere and sometimes your clients turn into your greatest competition. Whilst every industry is different there are competitors lurking around the corner in them all. It's all part of the game, it's what keeps you sharp, inspires innovation and your business needs it to stay fresh.

Building from the inside

Whilst there is nothing you can do to change what your competitors are up to, there are practices you can instil within your company that will help you keep up.

a.   Know the culture of your company

Culture is basically how you do things in your company. Culture is the value and practices of your company shared by the employees – from the way the phone is answered to how the employees respond verbally, in writing, in a timely fashion, how they treat each other and your customers. It is everyday life in your business.

When you start out, it's easy. There may just be you or a few others working together and you can lead the way by example. But as you get bigger, employ more people and are less hands-on, it'll be tougher. To be authentic, culture has to be owned and lived by everyone in your company, so it's not simply a list of rules and regulations.

You often hear companies say it's their people who make the difference. In a service offering, yes, it absolutely is about the people, but that's not enough. You need to build a culture where those people are supported and encouraged to be outward looking, encourage innovation, pursue excellence and work together. All this will help you stay ahead of your competitors and that is how the business is run on a daily basis.

b. Have a mission statement or credo that reflects the ethos of your company

One of the great things about a business plan is that it really gets you to think about what your company actually does, why it exists and what it means to the employees and clients. A mission statement is a formal summary of the aims and values of a company or organisation. It is a short written statement of your goals and philosophies. Perhaps this seems really obvious, but actually committing it to paper helps to get your ideas in order and then, as you grow, new members of the team will be able to capture your vision for themselves. It's really an internal document, rather than an external one. Anyone reading it should be able to know immediately who you are and what you do.

Here are a few examples of company mission statements to get you thinking:

Amazon's mission statement is 'to be Earth's most customer-centric company where people can find and discover anything they want to buy online.'

Tesco want 'to be the champion for customers, helping them to enjoy a better quality of life and an easier way of living'.

Apple on the other hand 'is committed to bringing the best personal computing experience to students, educators, creative professionals and consumers around the world through its innovative hardware, software and Internet offerings'.

If you're stuck for inspiration consider answering the following questions to get you thinking:

What do you do?

How do you do it?

Who are your customers?

What value are you bringing?

Your answers should form the framework for your mission statement and help you stay on track and focused.

c. Have a value proposition

A value proposition, on the other hand, is for your customers. It's a clear statement of tangible results a customer gets from using your products or services. Its outcome is focused and stresses the business value of your offering. Putting one together will help you see how you make your customers' or clients' lives better. It'll help you build your marketing messages and sales strategy.

To define the benefits you need to think about:

1. **What problem you're setting out to solve**. Charles Kettering, an American inventor, once said, *"A problem well stated is a problem half solved"* and many entrepreneurs make the mistake of diving headlong into the solution before really understanding the problem they're looking to solve.

2. Once you've ascertained that the problem needs fixing, ask yourself **what is unique and compelling about the way you propose to fix it?** Market research will go a long way here, as you need to think about your audience, what they want and how your service or product fulfils that need.

3. The last component is really all about you and **why you're the best company to provide this solution anyway**. This is the section that'll help you stay head and shoulders above the competition. By having a strong grasp on the competitive landscape, it'll be easier to position yourself in different way

A few value propositions from leading companies to get you thinking:

iTunes: You've never been so easily entertained. iTunes makes it easier than ever to browse and organise your music, movie, TV shows and more. Add to your collection. And play it all, anywhere.

HubSpot: Use HubSpot's Inbound Marketing software to consistently generate more visits, leads and customers.

Spotify: Let Spotify bring you the right music for

every mood and moment. The perfect music for your workout, your night in or your journey to work.

d. Have a vision statement

Be very clear on what you want your business to achieve, what the company's goals and objectives are and where you want to be in the future. A vision statement is all about the future, looking ahead and being aspirational; it's about where you're heading.

The **Chrysler's Group's** vision is 'to build cars and trucks people want to buy, will enjoy driving and will want to buy again'.

The **BBC's** vision is 'to be the most creative organisation in the world'.

The charity **Marie Curie** wants 'A better life for people and their families living with a terminal illness'.

I used to believe having these statements was foolish. I thought they were a waste of time, that people didn't believe in them and they were never taken seriously. However, through my experience, there have been plenty of times when we've lost our mojo and to get it back we needed to go back to basics. You need to have a clear sense of who you are as an organisation before you can conquer the world. Being truly focused as a team will surely help you get through the tough times. Having a clear vision will give you something to cling to when the waters get choppy.

e. Know your positioning

Knowing who you are, what you stand for and how you operate will give you great foundations for the future, but you also need to think about how your clients and customers view you in relation to your competitors; this is known as your positioning.

Where and who is your target market? Are you in a saturated marketplace where a lot of your competitors are also positioned? Who are your competitors? Are they advancing more quickly than you? Do they have a better quality of delivery? Are they more expensive or cheaper than you? Do they have a more creative approach in their products or service delivery? Are they advancing with new technologies? Is your portfolio of services good enough?

Questions, questions! Putting your business under the spotlight will surely help you focus everything you do. For us, every industry organises meetings or events of some sort, but we chose to focus on the life sciences industry. Within that industry, we have positioned ourselves as specialists offering a premium, white glove service; it means we're not the cheapest, but we can justify that through the 'added extras' we provide. There are other companies working within the arena who have chosen to position themselves as the 'most cost-effective' option, meaning they'll do the job for less, but you won't get the same service. There's nothing wrong with that – they've just chosen to occupy a different position in the market. Think of the supermarkets: Marks and Spencer's food occupies the high end, with premium products, pre-prepared food and a higher price tag. At the other end of the scale you have Lidl where you're never quite sure what brand of cereal they'll have in stock, but you can guarantee it will be cheap. M&S know their customers care about presentation and quality. Lidl know their customers care about price. When you know where to position yourself you can make sure that your products live up to your customers' expectations to build trust, repeat sales and business growth.

Managing change

From 2013-2015 I had somewhat of an awakening. As you know, we were a company built on passion and personal connections. When we entered the niche events market there weren't many others vying for business, so we could quickly gather pace as a small, personal company offering a white glove service. That was our position and we trundled along without much thought of what was going on, until it became apparent that work was harder to bid for, harder to win and clients were expecting more for less.

It was like we finally woke up, took a look around and realised this once sparsely populated land we owned was now overcrowded with rivals, offering more than us at better rates. It was a harsh wake-up call and meant we had to reassess our position in relation not only to our competitors, but also in comparison to the needs of our clients. The company had become stale, our competitors were doing much better than us, they were growing at a fast rate and their profits and margins were increasing far more than ours.

I knew in my soul the company was only going at a steady pace and it wasn't good enough in this fast progressive environment. As a leader, you have tough decisions to make all the time and this, for me, was another difficult one. But I could see everything slipping away so fast so I had the vision to bring in people to bring a freshness to the organisation, a new approach and a new vision on how the company should look and what we wanted to achieve.

We rebranded, we advanced with new technologies and restructured the business to suit the needs of our clients. We could see the amazing change happening, the freshness and energy it brought to the team. Our existing clients were reassured of our quality service and were gratified with a fresh approach more aligned with the coming times. But at the core of everything was a clearly defined mission, vision and value proposition. This gave our great team something firm to cling to as the changes took place around them.

We knew we were back in the game and we were now surpassing our competitors. We kept expanding our portfolio, going into different markets and services. As well as the expansion project, we were starting to look at acquisitions and replacement services – just like so many of our competitors had already been doing. This basically meant enhancing our own services and providing replacement services to help us achieve additional revenue quickly.

Let me give you an example. In our business, we are responsible for organising delegates' travel. However, we are not a travel agency – or at least we weren't. We used to outsource that function but we are responsible and accountable for its delivery and budget to our clients. So, to offer our clients an additional service and to boost our own revenue, we decided to become IATA approved and set up our own travel agency. We realised we were paying other companies roughly £300,000-£500,000 every year for a service we could provide for much, much less. So we now have a travel agency incorporated as MD Travel. Within the life science industry we're also very well connected, so we're using that to establish MD Recruitment to help place staff within the industry and keep us linked in with as many companies as possible.

Competitive advantage

So my words of wisdom in the competitive world are always have that competitive advantage:

a. Do it better

b. Do it differently

c. Gain customer loyalty

d. Build sustaining relationships

e. Keep the energy in your business

f. Motivate your team so they are encouraged to work hard, work hard and work hard

g. Make sure your team is a happy team – happy team = happy clients

h. Keep your eye on market trends

i. Watch what your competitors are doing themselves

j. Find out why clients work with them and not you

k. Always be ready to advance with new technologies

l. It's about partnership

m. Learn how to target clients

Thoughts to take away

Don't fear your competitors – they can really help you out. You need them!

- Keep your eyes open; competition can come from all over the place: direct competitors, indirect competitors, replacement competitors.

- Strengthen your company from the inside out: develop your mission and vision statements, think about your value proposition and what really makes you stand out.

- Build a strong culture that empowers your people to do their jobs well and encourages collaboration and communication.

Chapter V

Stick through the hard times – you'll become wiser

It's no coincidence that this chapter comes in the middle of the book. In a sense, it's what will make or break your business. Don't ever be under the illusion you will sail through business unscathed. But don't be afraid, either. Your business will be defined not by the way your profits rise, but by how you deal with the tough times. The rough patches themselves won't kill your business off, the way you deal with them just might.

As you well know, the power of hindsight is a great thing and if you can take the challenging times and appreciate what they have done for you and your business, you'll be far richer than you realise. I never realised the resilience I had within until I faced the greatest challenges of my career. When you care so much about your own business and the people you have working for you, you'll see you have an unfailing spirit to get through and keep going.

I've already shared with you the story of the £100k travel agent debt that left us within hours of having to shut up shop. But in terms of troubles that was just the tip of the iceberg. In the previous chapters I've encouraged you to think about your competitors and also your 'market'. When you're battling for clients it can be easy to take any job that comes along, but if you're going to stay true to your mission, your values and your team, then not every client is worth having. I've talked a lot about watching your back for competitors, but you also need to keep an eye out for the unsavoury clients; they, in a sense, are even more cunning and dangerous than the competitors.

As a word of warning:

    a.   Do not work with the bad payers

b. Do not work with the reputation destroyers

c. Do not work with the resource drainers

d. Work with the clients who appreciate the VALUE YOU BRING TO THEM

One of my defining moments as a leader was the first and only client I ever dismissed. Yes, you did read that right – I sacked a client. I refused their income and firmly closed the door on our relationship. They were based on the west coast of America. When we won our first project from them, we were excited and felt this could turn into a substantial account for us. I visited their offices in Los Angeles. Everyone was very pleasant and looking forward to partnering with us. We'd gone through the usual process of getting to know them, understanding their vision, confirming contracts, agreeing budgets and charting the course for the future together. We'd been open, honest and transparent, as always, and certainly weren't cutting corners – we'd learnt our lesson on that front!

Everything sailed on nicely for a few months and we were getting excited about working on our first event together. Then, one evening, I remember coming back into the office at about 9.30pm. I wanted to clear up a few bits and pieces before I went home. The office was quiet and I was there alone, apart from one member of the team who was working on the account for our new American client and stayed late because of the time zone difference.

This member of the team was usually bubbly, bright and enthusiastic, but I noticed she was a little subdued. I knew something was up and as I got closer to her, it was evident she had been crying. Naturally I asked if everything was

OK and she opened up about the conversation she'd just had with our new client.

As you know, part of our role was booking travel arrangements for our guests. As always, we aim to follow our clients' details to the letter and we'd reserved seats on the right flights as requested. But in this situation there had been some miscommunication. By law we're not able to specify which seats we can book in economy, the traveller themselves must book their own seat 24 hours in advance of departure. However, this client was under the impression that by 'reserving seats' we were able to book the very specific window seat she wanted. Sadly we weren't and she was not happy.

This is one of those situations where our hands are tied and there was nothing we could have done about it. Stacie, who was one of our best team members and had a wonderful way with our clients, had spent the evening trying to explain to the client we were only able to book *a* seat not *the* window seat she wanted. Misunderstandings occur, it's part of life. They're frustrating but sometimes you just can't see these things coming.

In most cases, you just have to appreciate there was a slight confusion, make what amends you can and get on with things. However, this client went wild. She was irrationally out of control. Not only had she verbally abused a member of my team and reduced her to tears, her colleague had then left a horrific message on my voicemail using foul language.

To top things off, she made her assistant (who was clearly totally embarrassed by the whole scenario and apologised profusely) call my home phone in the middle of the night just before our client departed on her night flight from Los Angeles to lay into us one more time. I was absolutely horrified with their unprofessional and shameful conduct. And let's just remember this was all over a window seat. A window seat, I ask you! We'd got her and all her colleagues and delegates on the flights they requested, with the right visas, at competitive rates with transfers and goodness knows what else; we'd just not been able to perform the miracle of getting her a window seat.

As ridiculous as it sounds, situations like these happen. I'm no longer shocked at the irrational response and behaviour of some people. Who knows what else is going on in their lives to make them explode over the tiniest of details, but you need to remember there's nothing you can do about someone else's conduct. All you can do is to keep your cool. Remember, there is a solution to every problem, and as the leader of your company your people are looking to you for direction.

By now you know that I only began to really step up when other people put their faith in me. When I saw managers who believed in me and encouraged me I wanted to step up and perform. Your people are so important to your business. It's one of those clichés that has come about because it's absolutely true. It's a big lesson I learnt early on and despite other things I may not have done quite right, I have always taken care of the people who make my business run. I had great respect for my team; they all worked incredibly hard and put a lot of their personal time and energy into the business. I made sure the culture of the company was to treat everyone with that same respect regardless of whether they are our peers or vendors. So I was dismayed that a client of ours would treat me and, more importantly, my hard-working team in the way that she did. Her behaviour and attitude did not fit with our culture.

In the immediate future we had no option but to fulfil our duty of carrying out the meeting in Paris – we were contractually obliged. I had hoped that by the time she'd got to Europe, the client in question might see the error of her ways. I made a special effort to be at the event myself to speak with her in person as I didn't want my team taking the brunt of our client's displeasure, but she was still so angry about her seat that she refused to even shake my hand.

I understand that people get stressed, business is tense and sometimes we all respond in ways we wish we hadn't – that's life. But you've got to draw a line somewhere. It was at that point I knew things had gone far enough. Our team worked hard, really hard, to organise great events for our clients. We always had a great atmosphere in the office where everyone pulled together and loved what they did. To see that great team demoralised and even reduced to tears just cut across everything we stood for. We had a great culture, a great ethos and this client was just breaking that down. This was not how I wanted any of the team to be treated and if this was the client's culture on how they behave, then it had no place in my company.

So I decided to fire the client. For all the income they would have potentially generated, all the events we were running across the world for them and all the revenue they could generate, they were also taking away our team morale, our confidence and our passion. I knew that was more important in the long run and it felt really good to stand up for my team. I could see they felt valued and appreciated because of my actions and their passion for the company grew.

In reality, what we lost in terms of revenue from the client we made up for in team spirit and camaraderie. It was a price worth paying ten times over. I made a formal complaint to the most senior person at that meeting, I told him everything that happened and ensured he listened to the abusive phone message. After returning to the UK, I went straight to the client's UK headquarters, met with the Head of Procurement and asked him to remove us from their vendor list. I also asked him to please send a note to everyone concerned in the company, asking that they never contact my company again. I duly provided him with the full details including my recorded messages and he was very taken aback about how we were treated.

As far as we were concerned, we'd drawn a line under the whole situation. We didn't want to be associated with a company that dragged us down so much. However, about eight months later, a few of our team were exhibiting at a conference in the US. I wasn't there myself, but two ladies came up to the stand and asked to speak with me. It turns out they were from *the unpleasant client,* as we'll call them, and they really wanted to meet me because everyone in their company heard they had been fired by us, their vendor. It was unheard of and, as a result, everyone in the company had had to undergo a short briefing about how to treat vendors and embrace them as partners. They were instructed to treat vendors appropriately and not just to use them as the scapegoats.

I was amazed! In my mind, once we were off the vendor list that was the end of our relationship, and that was that. Of course, I don't know what happened to the member of the team who was particularly abusive, but it was great to know that by standing up to them we helped to bring about a change of culture. I look back at my courage, bravery and audacity to dismiss a potentially enormous client, particularly in the early years of starting my business. Having a strong set of principles and firm belief in the value of your team will put you in good stead for whatever life throws at you. Never fear those kinds of decisions, be brave and always care about your team, your service and your business.

Dealing with personal challenges

It's also important to remember that the troubles that come your way won't necessarily just be professional ones. So often business leaders get labelled as being ruthless to the point where they abandon their families and eat, sleep and dream work – nothing else matters. This makes for great stories about power-hungry egotists – but it's not the norm. From my experience, you need your family and friends to keep you grounded. They're the ones that help you stay true to yourself. They're the ones who can tell you to stop, slow down and just pause. Sometimes they don't need to tell you, sometimes things just happen that make you.

For me it was my father's diagnosis with terminal cancer in 2008. My parents had been there for me throughout my career. They'd dried my tears as I'd struggled through my school years. They'd allowed me to spread my wings and enter the world of work, rather than pushing me into the world of academia. Those times when work was consuming my life, Dad had been the one to take me to the pub, sit me down over a pint of Guinness and tell me to take stock of my life and just slow down.

When Dad got poorly, there was no question about returning home to be with him. It was something I had to do. He'd had surgery at the end of October 2008 and I vividly remember receiving a call from my brother Niall letting me know the outcome: the colon cancer was incurable. It had spread. We were all utterly devastated with the news.

I went home to see Dad and he told me he didn't want to die in hospital. He wanted to be at home. At the time, my mother was being cared for in a nursing home with a form of Parkinson's disease. Mum had been sick for a number of years and by 2008 she needed 24/7 care in a nursing home near our own home in Claremorris, in the west of Ireland.

So there and then, I decided to leave the UK, appoint a CEO and move back to Ireland to care for Dad. It didn't take long to make the decision. I knew Dad would be with us for only a short time and each day, week and month were precious. It's at moments like this when you're forced to prioritise and there is no question about the outcome. This was the first time I faced death in my immediate family, but it's something we all have to come to terms with. Whether it's the death of a loved one, the illness of a friend or the breakdown of a relationship, life is full of personal battles that run alongside and intertwine themselves with our business lives. To try and keep the two separate is impossible.

So while I was in Ireland with my family, a member of my team had stepped up into the role of CEO. Again, it was a decision I'd made out of good faith, with the best of intentions. But, since this chapter is all about the trials and tribulations of running your own business, as you've probably guessed, things weren't plain sailing. I trusted the individual to lead, manage and deliver our services in the same way as I had. However, after 18 months at the helm, our profits started to fall and the healthy thriving business I'd built began to crumble before my eyes.

When my father lost his battle with cancer in 2009, his death left an emptiness inside me. Life changed. I changed. I found it difficult coming to terms with his passing and I had lost my spark, lost my passion and lost the desire to continue with the business. My thoughts were compounded as I looked at spreadsheets of our profits and saw that the company had not been cared for with the attention to detail that I would have given it. A part of my spirit had been crushed and the energy and enthusiasm I'd had for life and for my business just wasn't there any more. The fragility of life became so real, and as I saw my mother getting weaker by the day I was ready to pack it all in, wrap up the company and return to Ireland. I didn't have the emotional or physical energy to rebuild it. I felt the lowest I've ever felt. I just wanted out.

I even went through the process of selling the company and had a buyer lined up, but something held me back. By now, you know my philosophy in decision making. I believe it's better to make a decision than to be inactive and procrastinate. But if starting your own business is the biggest decision you ever make, then packing it all in and selling it is a pretty close second, and important decisions need to be made with a rational mind. I certainly wasn't in the right frame of mind to make any decisions so soon after the loss of my Dad. This is where your friends and family are so important. They know the real you and can encourage you to take a breath before you make the call.

Know who you can trust

So I decided to keep the business and rebuild the success we'd once had, but it turns out things weren't that simple. While I'd been with my family, the CEO in charge hadn't been running the business with quite the same care as I had. We weren't attracting new clients, figures were down and staff morale was also low.

It was around the time when offshore trusts had been bandied around as the next best thing. My CEO had suggested that we should pursue this option. Before jumping into things, I made time to investigate this myself and met with financial advisers to seek their insight and get the full information. They were charismatic, professional and captivating. They advised me to put *all* my company shares into a trust, assuring me that I'd remain in control while the company made profits. These advisers seemed reliable and honourable so I went ahead. What they did not explain in clear terms was that I was NOT the owner of my business any more. Clouded by my own grief, detached from the everyday workings of the business, and through my innate fear of finances, I had agreed. As the profitability of the company then proceeded to tumble over the subsequent months, I knew things were going terribly wrong.

I quickly realised that I needed to seek advice from my lawyer. I remember arriving at my lawyer's office and walking nervously along the corridor. What she'd unearthed was more than just financial mismanagement. By holding our shares, the trust controlled the company. So since the shares were now the property of the trust, so was my company. I was no longer the owner. Despite everything I had been promised, MD Events was not mine.

The blow hit me full on. I had been completely duped. I'd been advised by those I considered professionals that the trust belonged to me, I controlled it. That was always so important to me, as I'd built the company from my kitchen table. It was important that I decided what happened to it, I developed the culture and led a team in the way I wanted. But they never explained clearly that the trust controlling the shares also controlled the business. The wool had been pulled over my eyes during those vulnerable years in my life. I was devastated, but I was also angry.

As you know, this was a vulnerable time in my life and the urge to walk away and leave it all behind could have been there. However, amidst the stress of it all, I felt a huge sense of injustice. My mother had always run her business with such a high level of integrity. I'd followed in that vein, refusing to work with companies who didn't respect my team and now, when everything was falling apart because of the greed and lies of other people, I felt more strongly than ever that I had to seek justice.

Had I known the months and even years of legal wrangling it would take to right that wrong, perhaps I would have thought twice. But I couldn't be left wondering 'what if' or 'if only'. If I chose to shrug my shoulders and throw in the towel, I'd walk away with nothing, handing victory to the crooks. If I took those who'd lied to me to court and lost, at least I'd have tried and could hold my head high. Something inside me felt it could be put right. So once I'd made the decision, I set about my planned approach.

I appreciate now that I didn't fully understand the seriousness of the situation. I've since heard of numerous businesses who were duped into giving all their shares to offshore trusts, but at the time no other company had taken their case to the High Court. The case took two years and was escalated to the High Court in Guernsey where the trust was held. In business it's easy to take control of the things that are within your capability, but some things are completely out of your hands – this was one of them. I have to admit that there were times during the process when the stress was crushing.

We simply had to supply the facts and allow the lawyers to do their job. There was nothing we could do to influence the situation. All we could do was to watch and wait. The days, weeks and months dragged on and, as the lawyers' bills began stacking up, the stakes actually got higher and higher every day. The more we invested in the process, the more we had to lose. It's cases like this when you have to ensure that your business is built on integrity. You can't cut corners and you can't try and do things on the cheap. Ultimately, all you can do is be accountable for your actions.

After months when the stress became all consuming, I kept thinking why has no other company who've been duped like this set out to reclaim what's been lost? Are we mad? Is this just the worst decision I've ever made? On the day of the final judgment I'm not sure I slept a wink. I'd long finished going over the case in my head, I just wanted a decision so we could get on and deal with the consequences.

To be on the verge of losing everything I'd sacrificed so much for, to feel betrayed and foolish all at the same time and to endure years of waiting for a decision was soul crushing. Relief doesn't begin to describe how it felt to hear that we'd won. It wasn't necessarily a feeling of jubilation, more a sense that justice had been done and, after all, we weren't going completely crazy. The court ruled that we had been wronged and every single one of the shares that had been taken from us had to be returned. My business was still my business. The crooks hadn't got away with it. Whilst this was the first case of its kind, it certainly wasn't the last. We'd set a precedent and I know other companies followed suit in reclaiming what had been stolen from them. That feels good.

The whole process taught me a very, very valuable lesson about financial control. Perhaps it's obvious and you're reading this wondering how I could ever have been so stupid, but it's amazing how easily you can do it. When you manage a business you oversee everything, absolutely everything. The buck always stops with you so deciding where to focus your attention is a constant challenge. Of course you need to build on your strengths but, as I mentioned earlier, knowing your weaknesses is also vital. When you know your weaknesses you should, of course, find someone to help you, but you also need to help yourself. Making the time to get up to speed on the areas of business you find challenging will help you look at everything with a more critical eye.

Had I been more financially astute, I could have saved myself the biggest headache of my life. I still don't claim to be any good at maths, and I get all the help I can, but I know enough to take a more active involvement in the finances of my company. I'm much more proactive than reactive now.

Personal challenges

Whilst the battle to regain my shares gave me sleepless nights, it was the battle that then followed with the CEO which caused me most pain. As you know, I'd appointed a CEO in good faith when I returned to Ireland. During that time, alongside the decision to move the shares offshore, the company had made dreadful losses. Sales were down, there was no growth, no new clients and the CEO hadn't even visited our regional offices, not even once. Things just weren't working for anyone. So I decided to let the CEO go. It was clear that if things kept on going this way, sooner or later there'd be no business to manage anyway.

Intertwined with the legal battles, my own personal heartache continued. My father passed away in 2009 and my mother continued to be cared for full-time in a home. She had been diagnosed with Parkinson's disease, which meant that not only was she physically weak but her mind was also frail. There were times when she couldn't recall who either I or Niall were. To see your own mother look straight through you like a stranger creates such a sense of loneliness.

When I look back, the mother I remember is the cheerful lady in her work clothes, stirring the stew on the hob while effortlessly making conversation with her guests. As

I battled on through the court case, I gained inspiration from imagining that strong and beautiful lady. When she passed away in 2011, it was the end of what had already been a long mourning process. I was about as low as I could possibly have got. Everything I'd held dear and worked so hard to build was hanging by a thread. There is no way to prepare yourself for grief like that, you simply have to fight on.

With the trust fund case rumbling on in the background, I was also seeking advice from my lawyer about the next course of action for the CEO. As I was trying to get everything in order, the CEO I was trying to dismiss came in out of the blue and presented me with a lawsuit. I was shocked and stunned. We'd done nothing wrong, so where on earth had this additional blow come from?

As the story began to unravel, it turned out that while setting up a new iPad for me, another member of the team had got into my personal emails, saw the correspondence with my lawyer and tipped the CEO off. What I had hoped would be a relatively amiable split became the complete opposite. Had I been able to speak with the CEO first, I believe there could have been an alternative, but slapped with a tribunal against me and my company, things were escalated out of my hands. We had no choice but to take it to the courts.

It was throughout those 12 months in 2012 that I struggled the most. The Guernsey trust case was going on side by side with the tribunal. It seemed like I was being attacked on every front while I was trying to steer my own ship to safety. I was flicking from one court appearance in Guernsey to another in the UK just days later. Still grieving for my father and having just lost my mother the previous year, dealing with the rollercoaster of emotions was very painful.

I don't know how I got through, but if you ever think you won't be able to cope with everything life throws at you, let me tell you that you can. Amidst the chaos and despair that my life seemed to have descended into, I knew I couldn't crumble. I had a team of people whose jobs I was now fighting for and it took every ounce of energy I had to galvanise myself and keep going. I'd made the decision to keep the business, and that's just what I had to do.

Alongside the background noise of court cases and tribunals, I had some very difficult decisions to make about the business. Something drastic needed to be done because we just weren't making enough money to support so many team members. I had to make cuts and massive organisational changes, or we'd sink altogether. I decided to close the Manchester office and relocate those functions to our Bracknell office. This meant losing our budget, proposal and venue search teams and, most importantly, it meant losing some wonderful people. That's always what hurts the hardest – losing your people – but we had to make cuts or we'd run the risk of going under completely. Throughout I kept focused on our overall mission and the aim of building that culture I'd worked so hard to develop. I guess it's a little like pruning a tree to get it to bear fruit again.

It's at times like this when you can do your best to protect your team, and that's all. It was impossible to shield them from everything. No company that sees sales dwindling is a nice place to be and so, in addition to redundancies, we had several other people leave. Morale was low, debt was mounting and there were times when I wished I'd just packed it all in when I'd gone back to Ireland. I wished I'd walked away and let it all fall down.

But I'd made the decision with good faith and for good reason and so I had to find the strength to live out that conviction. I couldn't allow myself to fall apart because I had no one to fall back on. I was on my own: no business partner to take any responsibility or accountability for the business, and if I fell apart, the whole business would suffer. I had to put on a front that everything was OK when it wasn't. I couldn't count the number of sleepless nights, the worry and anxiety with everything going on. But there is always a way through. I used to say a prayer each night, believing God would not have put these challenges on my doorstep if he didn't believe I could get through them.

By February 2013 we thought we were finally coming out of the storm. We'd won the Guernsey trust case and the case the CEO had filed against us had also been dismissed, so we'd won that too. As the storm clouds parted, I desperately wanted to focus on the business and to start rebuilding. We still had a great team, great clients and a great model – there was so much to fight for.

New trials

However, the deceit around the trust case ran much deeper. We weren't just duped by the trust funds themselves, we were also duped by the financial advisers who'd so earnestly promised me that the company would remain mine, even after I'd surrendered the shares. After winning the shares back from the High Court in Guernsey, I embarked on a lawsuit against the ruthless financial advisers to get the money I had lost to them. I was not allowing them to get away with the deception and dishonesty they caused. There was even more trouble to come when I then discovered that my current lawyers were deceitful with their costs. They had been charging me twice and even three times as much as they should have been, and hadn't recovered all the shares from the trust funds anyway.

We had to bring in new lawyers, bring them up to speed on the situation, return to Guernsey and dredge up the case all over again. We were reliving the nightmare. It felt like reaching the top of a mountain only to turn the corner to realise you're only halfway there. With clear evidence and the previous successes under our belts it felt like we were pushing on with more than just blind faith this time. Three years later we had everything that was wrongfully taken from us returned and our loans had been paid off. We were completely done with lawyers' fees and court cases. Finally, the storm passed.

Strengthen your spirit

Looking back, I can still remember the anxiety that hung over those years, but I can also see a more resilient and even wise character developing through it all. If you think what you're facing is too tough, it's probably not. And when you've got through it, you'll realise you're a much better person as a result. Believe it or not, the trauma and stress we went through was all worth it. It's amazing what you learn about business but, more importantly, it's amazing what you learn about yourself. Everyone has the resilience and spirit within themselves to survive. Never doubt your own abilities and never ever give up.

Through the toughest times I simply had to prioritise. I broke the big issues into small decisions and managed each challenge, one by one. I also looked with the level-headedness of hindsight and made decisions about which areas of the businesses needed my attention and about the sort of people I wanted to entrust my business to. In a sense, we had the chance to start all over again. We put in place a business plan. We developed a defined mission and vision and a culture that everyone loves and believes in. We've been able to hire a fantastic Chief Operating Officer, Tarquin Scadding-Hunt. We know what the competition is up to and we've raised our game to offer new services, such as our travel agency and recruitment agency, to pursue innovative solutions. As always, we've got some fantastic people working with us and our energy is, most definitely, back.

In 2015 I could finally breathe again, restore my own energy and focus just on the business – my business. Back to basics never does anyone any harm and that is where we went. We are now growing, the changes in the organisation have brought a tremendous turnaround to the business, to the team and to me. Whatever life throws at us, we handle it with integrity and honesty. When you do, you need not be afraid of the consequences.

Thoughts to take away

The tough times won't kill your business off, the way you deal with them just might.

- Trust the right people. Sometimes experience is the only way we learn, but make sure you choose your team carefully.

- A little integrity goes a long way. If you've managed your business based on trust and truth, you can hold your head up high and face the difficult situations without fear.

- Don't forget where you came from. Keeping perspective helps you manage the tough times with grace.

- You're tougher than you think. Believe me, you can do more and cope with more than you can ever imagine!

Chapter VI

Have the right people in your business

As you can see, getting the right people on your team isn't just important, it's essential. Believe me, the world is full of all sorts of employees. There are those who are idle, those who think they know it all, people who pull the wool over your eyes, those who don't have any sense of care, morality, ethics or principles and others who are driven by sheer greed. To make your business succeed you need to have faith in people to empower them to spread their wings and use their talents, but you also need to temper that with some caution.

You might think you know someone, but in reality you don't. When you take people on you need to do your homework, and whilst giving them the space to develop, grow and excel, you also need to keep an eye on your business.

Now, if the hardest decision was starting my business, the second hardest was refusing to let it go, perhaps a close third was the decision to recruit my first member of the team. The fact is there are only so many hours in a day and only so much you can physically do as an individual. Even with all the outsourcing and benefits of technology, there are human limits. So if you want to grow your business, you'll need to take on members of the team. It's not something you can rush into or take too flippantly. After all, as an employer you're responsible for the team.

For me, that moment came after the first year of managing the business on my own. The volume of work started to increase and with only myself at the wheel, I had been covering both sales and operations. I knew if I didn't get support, I would let my clients down. Not only would I fail to grow, I'd also end up producing substandard work.

I learnt a lot from my parents and one thing my Dad drummed into us as children was to take responsibility for our own actions. By taking on another team member, that would mean taking responsibility for them, their mortgage, their family and their livelihood – and that was a scary prospect. I couldn't let anyone down. I had to be confident it would work, but it would have been impossible to grow without taking that risk of expansion. In the end, there was only one decision I could make if I wanted my business to grow.

Once the decision was made, the really tricky thing was finding someone to fill the position. Now this is where it's important not to burn your bridges. You may leave a company or finish working with a client, but I have always made a point of ensuring I leave on good terms. Even when I fired that dreadful client, I made a point of maintaining professionalism to the end because you'll find that industry can be pretty incestuous and you never know quite where or when your paths will cross.

So one evening, not long after making the decision to employ somebody, I got a call from Stephanie Paterson. We had worked together for a number of years at our previous company and always got on very well. She had the same work ethic as me, great working values and was always so warm and friendly. When she mentioned she'd been made redundant, my brain immediately set to work.

I do believe in fate and, of course, a little Irish luck, so that night I made the decision to ask Stephanie if she would like to join me on my venture, even if it was just until she found another job. If she didn't like it or it didn't work out there would be no hard feelings and she would go elsewhere. To my pleasant surprise, she said yes and her first day was 2 January 2003. I never looked back.

Stephanie was a fantastic support. She worked tirelessly, putting in enormous hours and throwing herself into the business with all the enthusiasm and passion I hoped for. We organised a lot of meetings from her spare bedroom, and within a few months we needed a third person to help us. My second employee, Jackie Ventress, came along in April 2003 and that prompted us to move to our first office in Bracknell.

I'd never longed after my own office or a name plaque on the door, but I have to say, it was amazing to see the business actually become something real and tangible. I was so excited to see the business really grow and become the mature professional company I wanted it to be.

Those early days as a small team were wonderful and I will always be incredibly thankful to Stephanie for the incredible part she played at MD Events. She was everything that a great employee should be: trustworthy, honourable and reliable. Her loyalty was overwhelming and the business would never have grown without everything she brought to it. Thank you Stephanie.

Stephanie, Jackie and the great team I have in place at the moment are living proof that there are great people out there who value the opportunity to work for a growing company that wants to succeed. I've had the privilege to work with a number of wonderful people who've brought unique talents and insight to MD Events. People often move on to even greater things and I've always taken great pride in playing a part in their journey.

It's important to remember your great team; they are a reminder not to settle for second best because, as I'll now share with you, there are all sorts of people out there you don't want to let within a mile of your business and they come in all sorts of guises!

When you think of 'company killers' perhaps what springs to mind is those who are blatantly out to screw you over. Indeed, you get people who fiddle their expenses, take advantage of the perks and even those who steal from you. But some of the most dangerous employees are those who start to sour the culture from the inside out – I call these the 'bad apples'.

As I've mentioned several times, your people really do make your business happen, so creating a culture where they can thrive and excel is more important than you realise. Several years into the business we were pretty established and things were ticking over nicely. I was in and out of the office quite a lot, keeping the team up to date and leading, as best I could, by example. But things just didn't feel the same. Where once the team were excited about projects, willing to get involved and keen to go the extra mile, I met with disenchanted, gloomy and unhappy people. Rumours began to circulate that the team wasn't happy, but for the life of me I couldn't think why. Nothing, as far as I could tell, had changed. Business was doing well, our culture remained the same, everyone was treated with respect and we still made time to have fun. I'd built the company with the basis of empowering people to do what they do best, so I was really surprised to hear the team had been moaning and complaining.

Whilst I wanted to turn a blind eye and pretend I had an office full of engaged, motivated and inspired team members, I couldn't deceive myself, especially as I knew it would have an impact on our client relationships. And when you're an employer you see things through a very different pane of glass.

To get to the bottom of things I decided I needed to be more present in the office and I also needed to ask some questions. After a bit of digging into this issue, I discovered there was just one individual who was really dissatisfied. If you ever put a rotten apple into a fruit bowl then, pretty soon, you'll find everything will turn to mush. In the same way, I could see dissatisfaction spreading across the company, so I knew I had to nip it in the bud.

There are often legitimate reasons for employees to be unhappy, but sometimes you just get people who like to moan! To be honest, there is no job on earth that is perfect. We all have admin to do, meetings to attend and everyone works hard. As an employer, you want to ensure you create an environment where people are safe, happy, well supported and given every opportunity to perform well. You can research salary bands to ensure your wages are competitive and make sure the benefits you provide are also on a par with – if not better than – the competition. But ultimately you employ people to work for you. You employ them to do a job, as advertised on a job description, for a salary they agree when they sign a contract. Some people simply think they deserve to be paid more for doing less and, it would appear, I had one of those in my business.

Once you've identified your 'snake in the grass', it's slightly more challenging to do something about them! Sometimes you do have to cut people a bit of slack. You never know what's going on in their personal life that impacts how they behave at work. Sometimes people get bored and sometimes they're not ready for the responsibility they've been given. Creating regular dialogue where people can share their thoughts and feelings openly with their manager should help to identify these scenarios, in which case you can give them some extra support.

However, sometimes you just get people who don't want to be there, and they are the real challenges! As a company I'd always made a point of keeping the team as involved as possible, and as it was nearing Christmas we were due to have an annual full company meeting where I got to speak to the whole team, which was about 40 people, face to face.

Senior management gave their presentations, we shared some great results and worked really hard to show our appreciation to the team and it was all highly motivational. I could feel that the mood was good, so I took the final slot of the day to share one final piece of important news with the team. I didn't want to highlight anyone, point the finger or cause any undue unrest, so I simple reiterated my gratitude for the hard work, dedication and great approach of the team. I took time to acknowledge individual talent and encourage their career development.

I then went on, quite openly, to share that I'd heard several rumours that people were complaining about their jobs. I had to make it clear that whilst MD Events was a great place to be, basically we all had jobs to do. They were jobs the team had applied for quite freely and, if they chose, they could leave any time they liked. We weren't a prison and we weren't holding anybody back. Everyone was welcome, but I made it very clear that the door was open for those who wished to leave. I was quite general in my comments, no fingers were pointed, I merely stated the situation as I saw it.

Amazingly enough, the 'bad apple' resigned a month later. I think she got the message. And, almost like magic, the team became themselves. The fun and happiness returned and all was well within a short time. So watch out for those people who can cause damage.

The slick salesman

You also need to lookout for the 'salesmen'. Now every company needs salesmen and women to bring in your new business. But beware of the salespeople who are great at selling themselves but bad at selling your business. We had one individual who was full of the chat. With his smart suit, quick banter and charming personality he managed to persuade us he should come on board, command a bigger salary than anyone else and work remotely.

I'm embarrassed to say we fell for every trick in the book – hook, line and sinker. After a few weeks, nothing seemed to be happening. He had no sales and no client visits scheduled. In fact, he had absolutely nothing in his diary at all. When we questioned him, he always had some quick reply to put us off the trail.

Finally, after a couple of months, I decided to ask our IT person to link me into his email account to see what was going on. There was nothing there. Absolutely nothing. Not one email had been sent or received for two months.

He had not been in touch with ANYONE, yet here I was paying him this incredibly high salary. I scheduled a meeting pretty sharpish – it wasn't as if he had any meetings to rearrange!

With evidence in hand, there was little he could do to talk his way out of the situation and admitted he'd not been doing his job. So I asked him what he had been doing with his time if he hadn't been working for us. I expected him to confess to having a second job or perhaps to siphoning off our business to build his own. In truth, I wasn't prepared for the actual answer. He confessed that for the past two months he'd been having an affair with his neighbour and that is where he'd spent all this time! All of a sudden I felt a bit like a priest in a confessional booth! This man clearly had a lot of issues he needed to sort out, none of which I could help him with. I dismissed him immediately.

Dig deep

We went through plenty of employees, from the absurd to the ridiculous. If you ever watch *The Apprentice* and find yourself gaping with awe at the bravado some of them display, let me tell you they are just the tip of the iceberg. There are an awful lot of blaggers out there who'll tell you they can 'smash their targets', 'take your company to the next level' and have 'an enviable record of being the best salesperson in *every* company they've *ever* worked for'. Some of them are blatant liars, others are deluded, but some are more cunning in their approach. Just remember that words are just words unless they are substantiated with actual evidence, so take up their references, question things that sound a bit odd and keep an eye on everything with enough attention to spot the bad apples and the slick talkers.

The thief

It can be hard to manage the bad apples and the slick talkers, but occasionally things get so complicated that you need to get the law involved. For a while we had a young woman working with us in our finance team. She'd been with us for four years and was quiet, pleasant and had aspirations to gain qualifications in accountancy. I have great admiration for anyone who wants to develop themselves and put in the hard work required to work and study, so we were keen to help her.

But for some people it seems that temptation is a little too much. One summer I was in Portugal and I got a call to say that $17,000 had been stolen from our account. The money had been taken out of the account slowly over time and where it had gone was a complete mystery. We gradually began eliminating the various options and it became crystal clear it had been stolen.

Only a few people in the finance team could authorise payments from the account, so the net closed in pretty fast. It turned out it was this assistant who had taken the money. Furthermore, over the course of the past year, she'd helped herself to the petty cash, with cheques to the value of $100-200 each day. Yes, it slipped through our finance department and, as you know, I've learnt my lessons when it comes to finance several times over, but whatever I could or should have done to keep a closer eye on the company finances, theft is theft.

This lady was caught red-handed, arrested and now has a criminal record. She was only 28 and that aspiring finance career will never amount to anything now. In a sense it was so disappointing, but it's amazing how people can be so easily tempted and so quickly give in to the urge of greed.

With all those lessons learnt I made very, very sure that once all my tribunals and court cases were done and dusted, I found a solid, dependable second in command with an impeccable record. I've now got in place a great COO, Tarquin Scadding-Hunt, who's highly confident and has talents and skills that complement mine. Tarquin's fitted into the business like a glove, has the focus and energy to accelerate the company into a different era and has been instrumental in turning the company around. So the good guys are out there!

It's so much easier to get things done as part of a great team that's built on trust, transparency and loyalty. We've still got our jobs to do, but it's amazing how fun it can be when you're all working towards the same goals.

Thoughts to take away

Look after your people and they'll look after you – just choose your people carefully.

- You need a team if you want to grow your business. Don't be afraid of sharing responsibility; your business will never grow if you insist on doing everything yourself.

- Give your people the space to flourish. Empowering your people to develop their skills and talents will make your business stronger and also be great for you.

- Check your references carefully. Not everyone is quite what they seem!

- Take time to thank your team for their hard work. A little gratitude goes a long way.

Chapter VII

Have a healthy work/ life balance

The work/life balance is one of those things you'll hear about constantly. I quite like the definition given by *worklifebalance.com,* which describes it as 'Meaningful daily achievement and enjoyment in each of the four life quadrants: work, family, friends and self'. It's not a rigid set of guidelines, but more an ideal to aim for. One size never fits everyone, and what works today might not work tomorrow as your circumstances change. I guess, ultimately, it's measured by the way you have pride, satisfaction and a sense of wellbeing in your life

If you can achieve this from day one, then good on you! The reality is that finding the right work/life balance is an ongoing struggle. When you're starting out it's particularly hard. Going it alone means you've got no one to share the workload or the stress. If a job needs doing, you've just got to dig in and get on with it and that often means making sacrifices. But you do need to make yourself accountable to someone, otherwise you run the risk of losing your business, your family or your health.

Fuelled by the adrenalin of running your own business can get you through to begin with, but your mental health, and indeed that of your team, should be something you're aware of constantly. Mental health is a bigger issue than many of us are aware of and it can have devastating consequences. It is estimated that nearly three in every ten employees will experience a mental health problem in any one year.

Here are a few stats to illustrate the extent of the problem:

Mental Health Foundation

1. More than 40% of employees are neglecting other aspects of their life because of work. This may increase their vulnerability to mental health issues.

2. When working very long hours, 27% of employees feel depressed, 34% feel anxious and 58% feel irritable.

3. As an employee's hours increase, so does their feeling of unhappiness.

4. The more hours you spend at work, the more hours you spend outside of work thinking or worrying about it.

5. Many more women report unhappiness than men: 42% of women compared to 29% of men. Women feel there is more pressure to 'juggle'.

6. Nearly two-thirds of employees have experienced a negative effect on their personal life, including a lack of personal development, physical and mental health problems, poor relationships and poor home life.

Health

I began as a business owner putting in all the hours I possibly could. I loved the thrill of the chase, the buzz of winning a client and the elation of completing a job well. The prize felt great. Every new business owner works their socks off in the first few months and years, but then comes the point when you've set a new level of normality.

Whereas you might have worked a 35- or 40-hour week as an employee, as a business owner 15-hour days become par for the course and before you know it, you've made a rod for your own back. You soon realise that you've built a model that demands you work crazy hours and then backtracking is hard.

For me, things were compounded by the fact that we had international clients and flying around the world was part of my job. A very nice part of my job, to begin with, but the pressure that puts on your body is unsustainable. I could never sleep well on planes, so I'd arrive at some far-flung destination and just get on with work. When you're running an event, you need to be the first one up and the last one to bed. You're on your feet all day and when it's over you're back on a plane to go through the analysis. Somehow you learn to manage your life and adapt but, sooner or later, things will catch up with you.

I remember one particular situation where I was getting ready to fly to the west coast of America for a pitch that could potentially win us a huge client. I loved the thrill of pitching and standing up and proudly presenting my company. I was also a stickler for precision, so we'd gone through our pitch over and over again. Flying all the way to the US for one pitch also seemed like a long way to go, so I'd also scheduled in a number of meetings with other prospective customers. It had been a busy few weeks before and was going to be a long journey and a long week.

The night before we were to depart, I woke up feeling very unwell, my temperature was elevated, I was nauseous, weak and fragile. My head was racing with so many things, so I tried to ignore it, get some sleep and presumed

I'd be fine in the morning. But morning arrived and I was much worse. Instead of staying in bed, the martyr in me drove me to get up, get ready and meet my colleague at the airport. In my head there was no option. I had to get to that pitch, which meant I had to get to the airport.

En route, I realised it just wasn't safe. The fever was overwhelming. I couldn't think clearly about anything. My mind was a fog. So rather than going to the airport, I had to make a diversion to the hospital. The doctors took one look at me and admitted me on to a ward. I was completely dehydrated and was suffering with exhaustion. The hospital kept me in for two days, put me on a drip and monitored me for the following week. I'd always believed that mind over matter was enough to get you through most situations. A good attitude and the strength of character to dig in had got me through in the past, but when it comes to your health your body calls the shots. In a sense I was lucky – a couple of weeks and I was back in the office. Some people run themselves so far into the ground they never recover.

Perhaps you might have thought this was a wake-up call for me – well, I was so focused I chose to see it as an inconvenient pit stop rather than a reason for a completely new direction in life.

Roughly a year later, I was in Ireland, staying with my aunt and uncle for a couple of days. Again, I felt the same thing happen. Fever came over me, I was absorbed with feelings of nausea and felt so terribly weak. My family took me to hospital and, just like the time before, I was admitted with exhaustion. I could only blame myself and my relentless drive to succeed, but this time the consequences were that much greater. At the time, my Dad was the local Golf President and it was his President's Prize Weekend. A weekend of celebrations was planned and my parents were so looking forward to including me, for once, in something they were really proud of. It was a rare family occasion and not only did I miss out, my parents were so worried that they gave up their weekend just to come to the hospital to see me. They knew what was really important and I deeply regretted putting them in that situation. I felt I let them down and let myself down.

Family

As you know, I learnt a lot from my parents. They were rocks for me when I was growing up, from helping with those poetry recitals to giving me the freedom to enter the world of work and supporting me through my decision to go it alone. Whilst you always get some people who survive against the odds, building a successful business without the support of your family is like carving an ice sculpture in the Sahara. It's virtually impossible. Your family are there to pick up the pieces, to tell you to slow down, to encourage you when the world tells you you're crazy and to remind you of what's really important in life.

When you're young and enthusiastic, adrenaline and sheer excitement often spur you on to clock up a ridiculous number of hours, without even realising it. If you're passionate and committed, you won't mind a bit. I absolutely LOVED what I did, I saw it as my hobby, I jumped out of bed every morning and couldn't wait to get started, but I allowed it to steal many moments of pleasure with my friends and family. I look back now and have some big regrets.

I remember receiving a call from my brother Niall when I was in some far-flung place about to jump on another plane and zip off in a new direction. "Would you ever just phone your Dad?" he said. It was the simplest of requests. A five-minute phone call home to check in with my family and make sure they were OK and yet, when life is running at 100 miles an hour, pausing to ground yourself is one of those things that just gets forgotten. I didn't mean not to call, I just didn't get round to it. I really wish I had.

Both my parents have sadly passed away and, regretfully, I wish I'd spent more time with them. I can't get those moments back now, they're gone forever. As I sat by Dad's bedside in Ireland, the success of my business brought me no comfort at all. It's a sad reality that for so many of us our relationships have to hit rock bottom before we realise what they actually mean to us. When you reach that state – as I did – clouded by the grief and the pain of regret, you find yourself wanting to throw away everything you've worked so hard to achieve. You come to resent it and run the risk of losing it all.

My brother Niall has four beautiful children and, disappointedly, I felt I missed out on their early years. Believe me, I'm trying to make up for lost time now, but I can't regain those lost years. Then there are my friends who I wasn't able to support through their own times of hardship. When one of my best friends lost her father to cancer, I chose to attend a client meeting in Paris rather than go to his funeral. Personally I can now see that was the wrong choice. It still haunts me today that I wasn't there for my friend at the lowest point of her life. It's regrets like this which I want to help you avoid.

It's good for business

The problem is, there's a huge paradox around the work/life balance when you're getting your business off the ground. You have to work hard to get things started – there's just no other way to get it off the ground. Hard work, of course, brings in the business and keeps your company afloat. However, an even greater good could be gained from pausing and giving yourself extra space and perspective on life – if only we'd make time to stop and consider it.

As you know, when I returned to the UK after the death of my father and mother, I wanted to pack it all in. My business and all my achievements brought me no comfort as I held the hand of my dying father and whilst watching my mother fade away too. What it did do, however, was give me the perspective to see how off the pace my business had got. Perhaps if I'd stopped more often or slowed the pace down to look properly at what was going on, I would have noticed sooner.

Another pitfall for so many business owners is the need to do everything themselves. Now, I'm not a micromanager, but I always had a sense that I needed to be at all the pitches and the important events. I never cultivated a trustworthy second in command who could help take that strain with me. Being a business leader means just that – leading! It doesn't mean you have to do everything. You can build a team to do the work and guide and lead them in the way they should carry it out.

When you're racing through life it's amazing how easy it is to just 'manage'. You get used to 'coping' with inefficiencies because, quite frankly, you don't have time to stop and consider a more economical way to go about things. You also find yourself compromising on your suppliers and taking the 'better the devil you know' approach, when there could be much better alternatives right on your doorstep. Slowing things down has all sorts of benefits, not just personal ones.

All this racing around impacts your team too. You set the precedent for them and, as I've said many times, when your team are happy, you'll get the best out of them. So it's really a wonder why we don't all just slow down a bit more.

Making the change

In today's world, it's harder than ever before. We never get away from the iPhones, the iPads, emails, phone calls, back-to-back meetings. Life never seems to switch off. And if we're not *switched on*, we fall behind. How unpleasant is that? To manage stress, I would urge you to find other goals. As an entrepreneur, like me, you're probably driven by something. You like setting yourself a challenge and overcoming it, so just as you set yourself business goals, set yourself goals in other areas of your life too!

As I learnt from my two trips to hospital, physical fitness and mental health are all intertwined so schedule exercise into your diary, sign up to run a marathon or train with a group of friends who keep you accountable. When my Dad passed away, I knew I couldn't go on to the same degree I had been. So, in dedication to my Dad, I decided to participate in my first marathon. I trained very hard for it and was delighted to have achieved the whole 26 miles, but it was the discipline of training for it that helped me most.

The hardest thing about exercise is simply getting out of the door, but as you build up a habit of going to the gym, running, walking or whatever it is that gets your blood pumping, you'll notice amazing results. Exercise automatically improves your mood and boosts energy, improves self-confidence and alleviates anxiety. After a while, you'll wonder how you ever had time NOT to do it.

Personal goals are harder to set, but even things like putting friends' and family's birthdays in the diary and making a point of celebrating them is a start. Set yourself a challenge to find a great present for your partner or a new restaurant to visit – anything that helps give you a little space from work.

Many people I know also benefit from having a mentor. There are so many reasons why mentors can help you when you're starting out. Not only can they provide really practical advice on how to get started, building in a weekly session with a mentor will also give you space every week when you can reflect on work, life and everything in between. It's a good discipline to start.

Like everything, there's no one who can take charge of your work/life balance but you. Family and friends can help support you, but you make the decision. When you own your own company, you call all the shots; no one can make the changes but you. I can't urge you enough to make your own health and wellbeing a priority. I didn't and nearly lost it all. So here are the helping yourself tips to supporting that work/life balance:

Mental Health Foundation

1. Take personal responsibility, do not always blame others or a lack of time, etc.

2. Try to work smart, not long. It is all about quality not quantity. Try to prioritise, do not get caught up in less productive activities, and keep your day structured.

3. Take proper breaks and get some fresh air.

4. Draw a line between work and leisure. If you need to take work home, set a 'stop' timeline.

5. Reduce stress through relaxation, exercise and hobbies.

6. Recognise the importance of protective factors such as activities and friendships. Try to ensure that these are not sacrificed to working longer hours. Please ensure your spare time is spent on protective factors.

7. Watch out for the snowballing effect of working long hours. Take account of hours spent worrying or thinking about work when assessing your work/ life balance.

Today, my life is very different. I'm pretty sure that had I pursued a better work/life balance from the start, my business wouldn't have suffered at all. In fact, I may have avoided some of the potholes along the way. Now, as a matter of course, I set aside time to incorporate more exercise into my day. I also participated in another marathon – the pink ribbon overnight marathon for breast cancer in Edinburgh, Scotland. Following that, I kept on training and did a 25k hike over the Mourne Mountains in the north of Ireland.

My goals aren't just fitness related, either. They don't all involve sweat! I've challenged myself to diarise spa weekends away with my girlfriends and spend time with my brother and his family. Visiting my friends and spending time with my uncle Joss, who is very dear to me, are also high on my to-do list now – they are all personal goals only you can set.

If you've got the passion, desire and hunger to make your business work, you'll do it. Just don't believe the lie that you have to go hard at it 24/7 to make it happen. Believe me, you are set to succeed with a good work/life balance.

Thoughts to take away

The truth is there is nothing in life but time. The key to everything is how you manage it.

- Remember that success is not just measured in financial terms. There's more to your life than income projections.

- Develop a schedule where you actively make time for your family, friends and other outside interests.

- Notice the signs of stress so you can take action, before you get ill.

- Make wellbeing a priority for your team too.

- Taking a break from the grindstone can help you gain perspective on your business and even realise more efficient ways of doing things.

Chapter VIII

You are a leader

Remember that girl at school who crushed her confidence so much that she couldn't even stand up and recite a poem in class? Was she a born leader? Probably not. So often we write ourselves off because we don't fit the mould of what society says a 'leader' is. Our only reference point is generally politicians or ostentatious TV personalities who seem so assured of their opinion and don't care what anyone else thinks. In my experience, those 'leaders' are not the norm.

When I was a child, like most friendly neighbourhoods, we'd say 'hello' to our neighbours as they would come and go. When you're little, you never really care what people 'do' – what matters is how they behave. As we get older we get hung up on labelling people and we often jump to conclusions when we hear the answer. The truth is, it really doesn't matter what you do, but the way you do it. Now this neighbour, Eugene Dalton, worked hard, really hard. We'd see him head out at the crack of dawn, scraping the ice off the windscreen of his lorry in the depths of winter. When we were children, Eugene was rarely home before our bedtime. He was always friendly, always took time to chat and was a true genuine loyal neighbour. He eventually set up his own business, which is going from strength to strength every year.

Eugene's calm stable persona wasn't necessarily one I'd associate with a leader of a successful business. But I realise now it's exactly what made him a great leader. His hard work ethos and personable character made him just the sort of person others naturally follow. We often think if you shout the loudest, make the most noise and stand out in the crowd, people will want to follow you, but when it comes to leadership, it's more about trust than shock and awe.

I'm not sure at what point I realised I'd become a leader, but I guess it was really the moment I decided to take my destiny into my own hands and start my own company. Looking back, I was leading my client's events, leading my suppliers and partners I was working with and generally laying the path for the future. The realisation only truly dawned on me when I took on Stephanie and physically had to show another person the way I wanted the company to be run. It was an immense responsibility: not only was she dependent on me to put food on her table, she looked to me to manage her time and indeed lead her. Had I stopped to ask myself if I had leadership qualities, the answer would most definitely have been 'no', but like many things in business, when you are forced to do them, you find the ability from somewhere. Experience is by far the greatest qualification you'll ever gain in business; the experience of being led by a great leader and the hands-on experience of doing it yourself. Whilst nothing compares to experience, over the years I've built up a good picture of what a great leader is. If you aspire to lead your own company, it's helpful to have some sense of areas that you could work on to help you get where you need to be quicker.

Purpose: I was relentless. The tenacity and fearlessness caught me by surprise over the first couple of years. You never know your own strength and I certainly did not realise mine. No matter who said otherwise, I was setting up my own business and I was going to make it a success. This is one of the most powerful qualities of a leader. The passion inside you as you live, breathe, eat and sleep your desire will be evident in the business, to your team, your clients and all those around you. Your team will look for security in your strength. If you give up, so will the people around you, so keep on going.

My purpose was most tested in the period where the business was wrapped up in court cases. It was starting to eat away at my own confidence and self-assurance, but as a leader, you can't let it show. You need to stay firmly fixed on the horizon, regardless of the storm that's raging around you.

Self-confidence: Being self-confident is an important tool. If you lack it, you lack leadership. Self-confidence is about your own self-belief and KNOWING you are doing the right thing. Setting up my business was, indeed, the right thing to do and I KNEW it! People often think self-confidence comes naturally, but for me it developed over time. As I was encouraged and given more responsibility, as others put their trust in me, so I trusted myself more. The moment of realisation came when my colleague Brian asked if I'd ever thought of running my own business. The moment when someone verbalises their confidence in you is more powerful than you know, so don't just think about your own self-confidence, think about how you can grow other people's too.

Humility: I have to admit, this was the one quality that took me most by surprise. It's also the quality which, in reality, we see least of in the figures that the world reveres as 'great leaders'. Perhaps that's because humility is so subtle and yet so vital. It really struck me when I saw the team at one of my events working so hard. Of course I knew it was their job, and I paid them to do it, but to see that they weren't just going through the motions, to see them pulling together to solve problems, go the extra mile for our customers and really put in the hours was really humbling. I saw them look to me for guidance, direction, control. I made a point of showing my gratitude and realising that they too are real people. Of course, there were the slick suits, the bad apples and the plain thieves who didn't warrant too much of my humility, but I've always made a point of taking good care of my team.

I've also come to realise that being a leader doesn't mean you have all the answers and it doesn't mean you're infallible either – and that's OK. I've seen my team respect me more when I've been honest rather than trying to bluff my way through difficult questions. You need to be aware of your own strengths and weaknesses and that means accepting feedback – even the stuff that's tough. Getting off your high horse means you can actually look people in the eye and see what's really going on. The best leaders can admit when they are wrong.

Positive attitude: Another great quality in a leader is always looking on the bright side. Believe me, sometimes that takes all the energy you can possibly muster, but it's essential if you're going to create a culture of success. No one wants to work for a boss whose glass is always half empty. The old adage that people quit their bosses not their jobs is so true, and if you can maintain your positivity, you're halfway there.

Now, like me you probably know people who are so happy about everything it just seems so fake. That's certainly not what I mean by being positive. To be an authentic leader you need to recognise when things have gone wrong and admit that you've made mistakes. You can choose to respond by getting angry, burying your head in the sand or by picking yourself up, learning from your mistakes and moving on positively. An optimistic approach will help you find solutions; a pessimistic one will lead you down the path of self-indulgent procrastination. A great leader makes the best out of everything.

I remember an occasion when one of our co-ordinators was working on a number of different projects at the time and managed to email one client but addressed it to the name of another. We always prided ourselves on our personal touch, so muddling up clients wasn't great! What's worse was that the client wasn't best pleased and complained to her manager. The co-ordinator was so distraught and so distressed that the issue had been escalated that she thought she was going to be dismissed.

As it happened, I was planning to be in the office later that day and our general manager called me to let me know what had happened. To see the co-ordinator so apologetic spoke a thousand heartening words about her attitude and work ethic. I could see she cared about her work, her clients and her job. It was a simple, honest mistake and I needed to make sure she knew that. When I arrived at the office, I went straight to her desk and said: "Isn't it great we are all human and not robots? I'm really glad you're human and working for us". That was all I said, but it was enough to show her that I saw the heart she had for the business and her dedication to her work. She's not forgotten that experience and, indeed, hasn't sent out an incorrect email either!

Respect: A lot of people think that being a leader means commanding the respect of your team and there are all sorts of false presumptions about what that 'respect' actually means and how you go about getting it. People often confuse respect and fear and think that if you go throwing your weight around people will respect you. That couldn't be further from the truth. In my experience, you gain respect by showing it to others.

A while ago I watched a programme about Sir Alex Ferguson, the former manager of Manchester United and the most successful Premier League football team of all time. Respect was most definitely something that Sir Alex had, but he didn't earn it by throwing his weight around, keeping his distance, barking at his team. Throughout his career he got to know everyone in the club, from the chairman to the cleaner, personally, and he treated them all with the same level of respect, regardless of their level on the pay scale. He knew the names of their children, their family and he made a point of stopping and chatting to them all. He realised the value of this, and it's something I've always sought to instil within my company too.

It is very important to treat everyone with respect: your team, your clients, your vendors. Every time Viv our cleaner came into the office, I always set a few moments aside to chat with her and find out what was going on in her life. It doesn't matter who you are, remember 'it is nice to be important but it is more important to be nice'. It's amazing what you find out about people when you take just a few moments to stop and listen. When you understand where people are coming from, it's so much easier to walk alongside them and bring them into your team.

Responsibility: One of the hardest things about being a leader is the realisation that the buck stops with you. If you're not prepared to take responsibility, you're not ready to start your own business and you're certainly not ready to be a leader. One of the biggest guidelines I would give is NEVER EVER apportion blame. Just as you can take the credit for an accolade your company wins, you must also take responsibility for every mistake your company makes. If you want it to be your business, you need to take responsibility for your team's behaviour while they are on the company clock.

Yes, people will get things wrong, they will make mistakes and lots of mistakes, and mishaps will occur over the years of you being in business. With very few exceptions, most of your team don't make these mistakes out of malice or mischievousness. You need to ask yourself is the team trained, is the team aware of change, has the team been kept abreast of updates they need to do their job well and is the right person in the right post? You also need to think about the way you speak to your clients: could they misunderstand something, are we being clear in our directions with our vendors? There are so many questions to answer before allocating blame, but when you stand in front of your client they don't care who did or did not do what; they want to know what you're going to do about it. Assigning blame won't save a client from leaving you, sorting out a problem with efficiency and integrity will.

Of course if there is a problem you need to get to the bottom of it, but whatever happens in your business, it is your responsibility. If we skip back to Sir Alex Ferguson and the world of football, the year after Sir Alex retired from the game most of the players stayed under the leadership of the new manager, David Moyes. When results started to dip and the club lost their grip at the top of the league, it wasn't the players who had to face the cameras and take the blame, it was the manager who took the rap and ultimately lost his job. It's the same in business: if results take a nosedive, it's not the sales team who goes, nor is it the operational people, it's the CEO! If you can step up to the plate and take full responsibility, then you're on your way to being a great leader.

Empower your people

To truly succeed as a leader you just can't do it on your own. A general has their army, a prime minister has their cabinet and a pilot has their crew. In the best teams each individual knows their role and has the freedom, space and support to do that job to the very best of their ability. As the leader you create the culture, the energy and the environment in which this can happen.

When I look back at the defining moments of my early career, they were moments where someone took the time to get to know me, saw skills I didn't even realise I had and gave me the space and support to use them. I was 'let loose' and was delighted to be empowered by my boss and the company to get on with my job. People learn far more from doing than just being shown – just make sure they know you're there for them. Micromanagement is not a style of any leader, it is the style of a controlling, manipulative person who mistrusts and has no confidence in their team.

Communicate

Perhaps it seems obvious, but by encouraging open channels of communication within your team, you'll avoid a whole lot of bureaucracy and internal politics. I've mentioned before the importance of establishing a firm culture that's owned and lived by everyone. You can't achieve this by building silos and keeping office doors firmly closed.

Try to lead a communicative team who can share constructive feedback, ideas and suggestions on best practices, process improvements etc. Build this in from the start and you'll not only be surprised how it limits the internal politics, you might also get some great suggestions from your people. You are still the leader, and you will still make the final decisions, but it's much easier to lead when your people get your vision and have a chance to air their concerns in advance. As long as your team understands why you made those decisions and the reasons are explained clearly, internal politics will be restricted.

Be grateful

It's amazing how a small 'thank you' can go a long way. When my uncle Joss retired at the age of 66, his company asked if he'd be interested in working on an ad-hoc basis, filling in for people who were off sick or on holiday. He declined – point blank. He didn't think about it, negotiate with them or even try and get more money. He just didn't want to work for the company because he felt they never truly valued their team. His overriding memory of the company was that nobody ever said those two little words with that huge meaning: THANK YOU. He felt unappreciated. As a result this company lost a great asset to their team. And I learnt the true significance of what 'thank you' meant to my uncle and, indeed, to every employee.

Thoughts to take away

A great leader has many qualities, they are within you somewhere deep down.

- Have a purpose. If you're excited and love what you're doing, your passion will be infectious.

- Take responsibility for the decisions you make and the decisions made within your company. This strength of character will give your team confidence that they can trust you.

- Communication is the key to so many things. Building a culture where information is shared will avoid Chinese whispers.

- Humility isn't often associated with leadership, but it's an essential quality that helps you show your gratitude and also realise, every day, the good things in your life.

MDE Services Group Ltd today

Today, MD Services Group Ltd couldn't be in better shape. Since we started trading, we've seen more than $220 million come through the business. It's hard to believe that from my kitchen table we've created a business that now has a head office in Berkshire and satellite offices in Philadelphia, Hong Kong, St Petersburg, San Francisco and Singapore. The team now consists of approximately 70 people who speak 13 different languages between them and have great skills in everything from procurement and negotiation to finance, graphic design and logistics.

We've made a point of learning from our mistakes and using them to put us into an even better position than before. In short, I'm running the business using the advice I've shared in this book and it's working! We're now using our global team to ensure we know our market better than anyone, not just here but overseas as well. We're out there keeping up with innovation, predicting future trends and have a great team who can deliver.

In August 2014 I finally found a COO for the business to whom I could entrust the day-to-day running of the company. Tarquin Scadding-Hunt has provided insight, leadership and management skills to help us strengthen the business from the inside out and develop that business plan which will give us a clear path towards the future.

Whilst we've polished up our offering, we've actually broadened our vision as well. The market is so different from when we began all those years ago. We're now able to offer more to our clients and have expanded our customer base too.

In addition to MD Events, our events management company that continues to focus on the life sciences and pharmaceutical industries, we support a whole range of industries. Through corporate events, destination management and incentives, we're helping a wider variety of companies to organise great events across the world.

We're also supporting our clients in new areas. Through MD Travel we now have a specialist business travel consultancy to help our clients manage their travel more efficiently and cost-effectively. In MD Recruitment we also provide additional support to help our life science partners to find the best people for their businesses.

Life continues to move at a rapid pace, so we've also brought in some great people to help us stay ahead of the latest trends and advancements in technology and innovation so we can offer the best solutions, tailor-made to the needs of our clients. We've been left behind before and we won't be left behind again.

Bringing everything to life is the wonderful team we have at MD Events. Just as I was empowered to develop my strengths and build my experience, so I continue to encourage my team to flourish and grow. Tarquin has really helped us to organise the team into a more agile group that can respond more efficiently to clients, has the power and support to make decisions and isn't afraid to do things differently. I'm proud of the team and of all they have achieved, but I think the best is still to come.

Conclusion

Thank you for taking the time to read my book. Somewhere within me I felt that all those good, bad and just plain ugly experiences I had could really be useful to guide those starting out. Once the desire was there, 'I just got on with it'. Like most things, when you make the decision to do it, it's not as tough as it seems!

My one aim is to get more young people starting to think about entrepreneurship in a different way. We have so many false preconceptions and I wanted to let you in on the reality of owning and running your own business. I wanted to openly and honestly share the ups and downs, the excitement and the frustration so you can see what can be achieved with a dream and some hard graft. I hope this book helps to dispel some myths and even inspires you to think differently.

Of course challenges, risk and uncertainty are all par for the course, but they're not something to be feared. Think about your future, your ideas, your creativity, your imagination and your ingenuity, and don't be afraid to go forward. You have all the qualities you need to succeed within you; you'll only ever discover them when you put yourself to the test.

So dream big, never let anyone convince you that you can't do it. Take the step and just get on with it – who knows where you'll end up.

About the Author

Miriam Dervan is the founder and CEO of MDE Services Group Ltd. She is the CEO of MD Events Ltd, a leading global life sciences and corporate specialist meeting planning and patient service agency. She is also the founder and CEO of MD Travel and MD Recruitment.

Miriam's career spans over 25 years in the clinical research arena. She started MD Events Ltd from her bedroom in January 2002, growing it into a multimillion dollar global organisation that has managed more than $220 million since it was established.

Miriam is from the town of Claremorris, Co Mayo, in the west of Ireland, where she was raised along with her brother Niall. Describing herself as a non-academic, Miriam did not attend university but went straight into the working world from school. She started her career within the pharmaceutical industry with the Institute of Clinical Pharmacology in Dublin, working in the data entry department. Miriam then moved to work for the Irish Pharmaceutical Healthcare Association and Wyeth Laboratories along with a number of contract research organisations before founding her own company.

Since then she's travelled the world gaining immense experience in business management, cultural diversity and leadership. She has long been a champion and thought leader for women in business and women-owned businesses. She is on the European Women's Enterprise Council, which plays a big part in supporting women in business. Through everything she does, Miriam is passionate about entrepreneurship and her desire is to encourage free enterprise amongst pupils, students and young people in business.

Lightning Source UK Ltd.
Milton Keynes UK
UKHW02f1022121217
314239UK00006B/126/P